SAPPHO'S
LYRE

SAPPHO'S LYRE

Archaic Lyric
and Women Poets
of Ancient Greece

TRANSLATIONS,
WITH INTRODUCTION AND NOTES,
BY DIANE J. RAYOR

Foreword by W.R. Johnson

UNIVERSITY OF CALIFORNIA PRESS

Berkeley   Los Angeles   Oxford

University of California Press
Berkeley and Los Angeles, California

University of California Press, Ltd.
Oxford, England

© 1991 by
The Regents of the University of California

Library of Congress Cataloging-in-Publication Data

Sappho's lyre : archaic lyric and women poets of Ancient
  Greece / translations, with introduction and notes by
  Diane J. Rayor ; foreword by W. R. Johnson.
      p.   cm.
    Includes bibliographical references and index.
      ISBN 0-520-07335-5 cloth; ISBN 0-520-07336-3
      paper (alk. paper)
      1. Greek poetry—Translations into English.   2. Greek
  poetry—Women authors—Translations into English.
  3. English poetry—Translations from Greek.   4. Women
  and literature—Greece.   5. Sappho—Translations,
  English.   I. Rayor, Diane J.
  PA3622.R39   1991
  884'.01089287—dc20   90-48642
                                              CIP

Printed in the United States of America
9 8 7 6 5 4 3 2

For my mother and father

Contents

Foreword

Thanks mostly to Horace, some of the spirit and much of the letter of Greek lyric, though not the lyrics themselves, had both fame and influence in European culture even before the Greek language and its extant literature were recovered for Western Europe. Its favored motifs, its rhetorical strategies, its dynamics of transition, modulation, and "sequences of aspects," its spectrum of appropriate masks and the plausible situations of sung discourse, all the formal and thematic materials that Greek lyric poets had developed, were passed on by Horace to his medieval heirs (admittedly in ways that the Latin language and the Roman poet's genius had inevitably deformed and transformed) and thus entered into the lyric traditions of Europe even before the fall of Byzantium and the return of Greek to Rome. Thus even before the Renaissance something of Greek lyric had begun to be domesticated, and during and after the Renaissance that process of appropriation steadily flourished until, by the time Romantic Hellenism was in full swing, Greek lyric was familiar to Europe, had come to seem to be not merely the origin of Western lyric but also its enduring core, of its essence. There is not a little truth to this version of the place of Greek lyric in the lyric of the West, but that truth tends to obscure other aspects of Greek lyric that are no less important for its appreciation.

The verses in this volume are distinct from other collections of lyric poetry in numerous ways, but in two particular ways they are especially different. First, in their initial function: whom the poets wrote for, and, early on, sang their poems for, what their audiences wanted from these poems and apparently got from them; second, in what became of Greek lyric poems: how they entered the European lyric canon (to the extent that they did) and what their later fortunes tell us about them and us.

To the audiences for all the poets in Rayor's table of contents, but in particular for the audiences for the first nine or ten poets on that list, the readers of this volume would seem at best barbarians. Most of them, if male, were, had to be, skilled soldiers and athletes, and not a few of them, male and female alike, played stringed instruments well enough to perform at the drop of a hat before an audience of peers with rather high standards, accompanying themselves as they sang either songs to which they might possibly have written both music and lyrics or the golden oldies which they and their audiences knew by heart (as many of them knew, almost by heart, vast chunks of what we call Homer—and his rivals). The fact that most of us do not have numerous physical and intellectual skills of a high order and a high polish, the fact that, truth to tell, most of us are pretty narrowly "specialized," would seem to them to indicate that, radically deficient as we were in the aristocratic versatilities they gloried in, whatever our legal status, we were essentially slaves, fit only for a few simple chores, badly educated, clumsy, unable to protect ourselves, totally useless when it came to sailing a tricky ship in a Mediterranean storm, ignorant (most of us) of the gods and their ways—so which of them would want to invite many or any of us to a symposium? We would seem to them not merely inferior and uneducated and conventionally barbaric, we would sound to them—well beyond the primitive or the savage—barely human.

These people who would dismiss us without a second glance once they'd got an accurate sense of what we do, what we're like, what we value are the *we* (our crowd) to whom all others are *the others*. Even if they are not quite aristocrats themselves, by birth or wealth or both, they are attached, if they matter at all, to aristocrats, and even if they are not first on the guest list or even very high up on it, they belong, however tenuously, to the happy few, and they will end up at the symposium that would have no room whatever for you and me (it's not even clear that incompetents like us would be trusted to brush away the crumbs, much less decant the wine or pass the fruit). Being at the symposium (the male version or the female version—*these* opportunities were nearly equal) means that you do get to hear Sappho or Alkaios or Anacreon sing their poems, which means that you are considered fit for the sort of sharing of the cultural codes that these highly beautiful, very exciting recreations of it furnish to the members of the clan, the faction, the elite to which you happen, somehow, tightly or loosely, to belong. And sharing the cultural codes, learning to imagine them better in these beautiful versions of them, possessing them ever more profoundly and thoroughly as you learn more of them in the company of these people, like breaking bread with them or sharing wine with them, dancing and singing with them, worshiping the gods with them, laughing and joking with them, making love to them, fighting sometimes alongside them (and occasionally against them) means that you are one of them. It is at the symposium and at other gatherings both secular and religious that you reaffirm and deepen your sense of being part of this city or, more exactly, part of this group, this clan, or this fellowship that claims to be the city's center, to be at the core of its legitimacy, vitality, and prosperity.

The giving and getting of pleasure is one crucial aspect of the songs that were sung at symposia (or other gatherings, including those of a specifically religious character), but the pleasure is fused with something else. It is not so much information (this poetry is not didactic in the modern sense of the word), but rather a sort of display and reminder of the group's cultural repertoire (and treasury), of the values it espouses and the values it rejects. Being there, sharing the company and the wine and the dances and the songs is a way of professing one's civic (in Greece, this means one's ontological) identity, of confirming and validating (through repetition and renewal) one's right to be with the group and in it and have pleasure with it, of reassuring oneself (particularly if the pressures of the day, war, family squabbles, money troubles, have been specially hectic) of one's self, of who one is and what one lives for. (Having thusly described Greek archaic symposia and their aristocratic participants and the function of poetry in them, I become aware that this description sounds not very unlike one that could maybe be given of certain neighborhood bars, across the length and breadth of America, with country-and-western on the jukeboxes; and I think that's how, in not a few ways, the archaic symposia were, only much, much more so.)

They were, then, these archaic audiences and their poets, not surprisingly, the prototypes for Nietzsche's Overmen. Energetic, ferociously self-assertive and aggressive and competitive, sensual, gregarious, curious, passionately verbal and aesthetic and legalistic, they were at once nourished by the venerable, intricate, and powerful culture that Homer's epics give us some sense of, and themselves called upon to assist in the shaping of a new culture—that violent remaking of Greece that would produce the democratic polis, the Greek Mediterranean and its colonies, the pre-Socratics, the Sophists and the beginnings of Western science and medicine, Western rhetoric and historiography, Athenian tragedy, Greek art—and on and on. How much their being part of this explosion and violent reconfiguring may have contributed to the nature of their poetry (what the audiences expected, what the poets gave) or to its peculiar bite and tang, its elegance and its precision, would be hard, given the fragmentary evidence we have, to decide; but it would be equally hard to deny that such turbulent change and such extraordinary varieties of experience would have left little or no mark on the poetry that was contemporary with them. For our purposes, what we need to bear in mind is some picture of these wild and also refined aristocrats, caught in a severe cultural earthquake, losing one world, gaining another.

In their original context, then (which we cannot, of course, wholly recover but which, equally, we ought not and cannot ignore) these poems are a call to community, or, more narrowly and exactly, to fellowship, to fraternity and sorority: Live up to our ideals, strive always to be the person who is worthy of the high and holy and beautiful truths we value, strive always to become that person who is worthy of what we all strive to become. Outside their original context (and this would later become as much a problem for democrats and monarchs as it would be, fatally for the poems, for Christians and other puritans) the songs seemed to be a call to an individualism so radical as to be little short of anarchic, a ferocious adumbration of the counsels of Thélème: Become what in fact you are, what you want to be, do as you like, take what you want, enact your desire—for what you desire, you are. Nietzsche, then, while he got the context almost right, nevertheless—Romantic that he was—got the message as wrong as had those perverse Christians themselves, his archenemies. Those strong archaic paragons of individuality (of unfettered *voluntas*) had owed much of their strength to their groups and to the symposia and songs that both symbolized and rendered actual this configuration of passionate volitions in their unities (and, of course, the strength of the groups had, in reciprocity, depended on the strength of the forceful individuals who composed it).

Such extraordinary (in a sense, fabulous) people, though losing old worlds and inventing new ones, were seldom unequal to what their eras demanded of them—not only because of their own force and the force of their fellowship but also because they were sharers in a yet larger dynamic unity. They knew, after all, that they were part of Nature, which meant that they were somehow the kindred of the gods. They had to die, of course, and that was tragic, and in that they were clearly unlike (this was the big difference) their celestial ancestors. But ephemeral though they were, they had their time in the sunlight, which meant, mysteriously, that they had their own portion of eternity. The light they looked on and that illumined them, their prowess in battle or in the stadium, their beauty, their wisdom and wit, was a light they shared with the gods. The divine was everywhere. This all seems more than a little naive to most of us now, and maybe even a little primitive and Romantic to boot ("Hellas, the childhood of mankind"), but superior as we may, in some moods, be tempted to feel toward them because of it (and, in some moods, envious as well) it is the world-picture that informs everything they did and were, including their symposia and the poems that were central to their symposia. We have to remember that for them the carnal and the spiritual were, if not in fact identical, interdependent. They were, after all, as we used to say, pagans.

And that is perhaps the fundamental reason (the last straw, as it were) for this collection's consisting mostly of fragments. But to blame the Christians entirely, just because they invented the pagans, would be, though satisfying, simplistic, and it would get us ahead of our story. The Christians had had help; others had done their spadework for them.

To achieve genuine permanence in the canons of ancient Greek or ancient Latin literature, one of the surest ways was to find one's way onto the reading lists of Advanced Rhetorical Training (very roughly equivalent to our high schools, as they used to be). Failing that, it sufficed—or may, for a long while, have seemed to—to have got a place in the Alexandrian Library (or one of its rivals), to have been edited by its scholars and to have been placed on the shelves that various scholars came to investigate for various purposes. To have been included in the collections of common readers was better than nothing, but fashion here is less kind and less faithful than it is in libraries and pedagogies, so it was in the repositories of the institutions that fame or mere survival was best secured. But there were drawbacks even to being "preserved" in these stable and powerful sanctuaries of national culture, and all of the poets in this volume, alas, encountered them, both the lyric poets and the women poets—and, of course, since they were twice vulnerable, the women lyric poets.

What fitted an author for canonization on the syllabus of the Higher Rhetoric (in any of its changing incarnations) was beauty of language in combination with beauty of moral and patriotic sentiment: the object of education (here one is tempted to speak of a Greco-Roman tradition) was an eloquent good citizen—that is, one who could be eloquent as the occasion demanded, but, more important, one who could appreciate eloquence, one who could listen to and understand rational argument that rhetorical art had polished, organized, and clarified (it was understood then, as it is not now, that logical, rational argument, for various reasons—and not just for its rarity—is inadequate for civilized life: *ratio atque oratio*). Teachers of eloquence (whom, if truly suited to their vocation, beautiful language, not beautiful morals or beautiful jingoism, obsessed) showed a strong inclination to stretch the meanings of "moral" and "patriotism" to their snapping points in order to smuggle into the curriculum some gorgeous chunk of verse or prose; but they found it, by and large, almost impossible to include the lyric poets in the literature their students were required to analyze and memorize and imitate until its images and cadences were as much their own as their blood and their bones and the air they breathed. The Latin rhetors managed to get the lyrics of Horace into the sanctuary (the great master of protean irony scattered with lavish hand pious and civic-minded bromides whose wicked and wonderful indeterminacies a sly rhetor could deftly sweep under the rug, and besides, he was preeminent in very safe genres: moral satire, moral philosophical *causeries*, the *Epistles*, and, last but hardly least, moral literary theorizings). But Catullus, who eventually almost encountered oblivion, apparently had to entrust his destiny, more and more, as the centuries, first pagan, then Christian, devolved, to a few sagacious readers, to the happy few. The Greek rhetors rescued the victory songs of Pindar, nearly incomprehensible as these intricate, dazzling contraptions had become by the time various kinds of barbarians (the Romans among them) were learning Greek; whatever their obscurity and blinding beauty, they had plenty of locker-room wisdom to dispense: how to fight the good fight, how not to savor one's victory overmuch, and so on. But by and large, the lyric poets were not capable of being saved, lovely though they were, because their language seemed too difficult for people—even for those born with Greek as their native tongue—who felt they had enough to do to master the antiquated (dead) Greek of Periclean Athens (and learn enough Homeric Greek to dip from time time, as a gentleman ought, into those precious and *long* epics) without squandering energy and time on the dialects employed by the lyric poets.

That was sufficient excuse for not reading them, but the deeper reason was that their major themes and sentiments were often erotic. Pubescent males hardly needed to be encouraged to think about sex, and they certainly did not need to hear what the lyric poets had to say about sex: It is an absolute and very dangerous form of insanity, love is (but it's Divine, and it's Fun); birds and bees do it, do it; do it as often—well, use your common sense—as you get the chance: CARPE DIEM! Even when patriotic themes and religious pieties were interspersed in the lyric scrolls, somehow the more mature messages got lost or garbled, and what the young readers tended to really learn by heart was, of course, the celebration of the sweetness (and the adventure) of desire. So, by virtue of a "simultaneity of multiple causes"—their genre itself, its archaic dialects, its essential uninterest in the topics and emotions dear to the heart of what Gertrude Stein called "patriarchal poetry" (marching songs and very restrained hymns are central here), its tendency to focus on the truth and beauty of Eros, its obvious preference for feelings over logocentric and phallocentric dogma—for all these reasons, both separately and in their delicate and powerful configurations, the lyricists could not find permanent or secure habitations in what was the core of the canon: what advanced students of rhetoric read and absorbed and founded their mature careers and identities on.

As for the women poets, let alone the female lyricists. . . . If it was a question, and it definitely was, of finding for the reading list verbal and moral role models, of what use could women—even of women of genius who had somehow found real rooms of their own—possibly be to those young (impressionable, tender, malleable) males? Wasn't it rather odd—one might even call it freakish, rather "like teaching a dog to dance on its hind legs," as a later and very great rhetor would put it—for a woman to be able to write, to *want* to write, to write *well*? As for Sappho, even Sappho? She was, it seemed, in a class by herself (a gender by herself? that would resolve the problem maybe), but even she was, or especially she was—something of a monster, no? Common readers might like her, connoisseurs might single her out for the highest praise (it's to two of them, Dionysius of Halicarnassus and Longinus, that we owe two of our most extensive pieces of her poetry), but that "unofficial" approval could hardly secure a place for her in the canon that mattered, the canon that determined which texts would survive and which would not.

Her official survival was, one gathers, unthinkable. Even before the Christians got their hands on her (gradually some Christians would stop believing that the culture of their ancestors had been devised by Satan—but by then most of the real harm was done) her fate was sealed. (And if her poems were to be condemned to nothingness, it was not likely that those of her brother lyricists, much less those of her sisters, lyric and nonlyric alike, would meet with better luck.) But the qualities that had counted against lyric poets and women poets when patriarchal pagans were separating what helped their societies from what, they supposed, might harm them became utterly (not randomly) fatal when they were passed on to the Christian censors of the celestial patriarchy. What had been, in these poems, merely subversive of the ideals and habits of the good citizen in the eyes of the secular guardians of virtue became damnable in the eyes of their religious successors, damnable and combustible, demanding an auto-da-fé.

The legends about the burnings of Sappho's poems are, doubtless, mostly legends merely (for a sample of them, see C. R. Haines, *Sappho: The Poems and the Fragments* [London and New York, 1926], 5–6; for a lucid dismantling of them, see Edith Mora, *Sappho: Histoire d'un poète* [Paris, 1966], 145–50). But where, in matters such as these, there is smoke, there is usually some fire, even if it is essentially symbolic. If Gregory VII did in fact burn her poems publicly in 1073, his act—it was more than a gesture—was hardly intended to get rid of her for good and all, since he was doubtless not silly enough to think that he was destroying the only remaining copies of the Poetess from Hell; rather, lacking an Index (but not the germ of the idea of it), he was sending a message, to his contemporaries and to the future, about this evil and the other poetic evils of whom she herself was symbolic (as is frequent in such matters, this was a symbolic burning of a symbol). He did not, however, include on his bonfire the many and variously charming pornographic epigrams that were available in both "classical" lan-

guages in various collections (not least *The Greek Anthology*, whose lubrici-
ties are not completely camouflaged by being sandwiched between diverse
edifications, many of them pious); he did not set his torch to Martial, very
possibly the supreme artist in elegant porn (who has, here as elsewhere, the
eye and the hand of a premier diamond-cutter). Porn verse probably didn't
worry him much, probably because its banality is transparent, and (so he
might have thought) it attracts only the depraved and the unregenerate (let
the swine swim in their filth). But for eloquent erotics, for erotics that sing
their way into the very soul, for erotics that tell the self to have reverence
for its desire, for its hope, for carnal joy, that teach the self to love the self
and the world it has come into—what but the flames lit by hand and will
of God could annihilate that exquisite, nearly insuperable evil?

Jane McIntosh Snyder, in her excellent *The Woman and the Lyre: Women
Writers in Classical Greece and Rome* (Carbondale and Edwardsville, 1989),
tends to minimize the importance of the burnings: "A much more serious
problem connected with the preservation of Sappho's work (not to mention
countless other books of classical literature) seems to have been the decline
of learning and scholarship during the sixth through the ninth centuries;
Sappho's poems—along with the works of other ancient authors—were de-
stroyed, it would seem, not so often by fire as by neglect" (p. 10). Fair
enough: except that this view doesn't take into account the many "other
books of classical literature" by many "other ancient authors" that were *not*
destroyed (the "neglect" was hardly uniform, as her own qualification shows
and as can be seen in the collection edited by Warren Treadgold, *Renaissances
Before the Renaissance: Cultural Revivals of Late Antiquity and the Middle Ages*
[Stanford, Calif., 1984], 75–98, 144–72), nor does it offer sufficient ex-
planation for what seems to be, beyond the heartbreaking virtual disap-
pearance of Sappho herself, the most bitter and the most genre-specific of
the many losses, namely that of all the lyricists (except Pindar at his most
civic-minded) and of all the women. When Manuel Moschopoulos (see
Mora, 149), who was the last of the Byzantines to cite Sappho, made his
escape from the ruining city to Italy, why didn't he take, among the books

he managed to rescue, some volumes of Sappho (or Alkaios or Anakreon or any of them)? Because he didn't care about her or her fellow lyricists? Or because, as I think likely, there were no volumes of them immediately to hand? There were none that he could, in his desperation, swiftly snatch up and dash off with to the ships because of a neglect that was in part deliberate, because of a neglect that the symbolic burnings had called into being and had (by the power of legend) fostered. The manuscripts of Sappho and her fellows were few and far between; only the happy few knew them, and only experts, who might or might not admire them, consulted them, not infrequently not for strictly literary purposes. So what few copies of these (shall we say it?—amoral) poets the pagan prigs and fanatic Christian mobs (and the mice and the Popes) had not destroyed, the Venetians and then the Turks accidentally and randomly did. (The story of the émigrés in flight, to Crete and to Italy, and of the texts they managed to take with them, as well as the frantic search for Greek manuscripts in the Near East in the years immediately after the fall of Constantinople, is adroitly sketched in the opening chapters of Deno John Geanakopolos' *Greek Scholars in Venice: Studies in the Dissemination of Greek Learning from Byzantium to Western Europe* [Cambridge, Mass., 1962].

And that tells us some truths not so much about officious and official prigs, both pagan and Christian, or the habits of innocent mice and guilty Popes (or of Venetians and Turks) as about the nature and the power of lyric poetry and about our own divided hearts. What happened to Greek lyric poetry is, in a way, the aftermath of a curious chain of sad contingencies that will not (at least not identically) repeat themselves again. But the unique (and almost unbelievable) destiny of the poets who are represented in this volume of Rayor's translucent, richly visual and richly vocal renderings of them should perhaps set us to pondering, better than we mostly do, both the incomparable nourishment that it furnishes the human spirit and its extraordinary vulnerability in a world that rarely knows what is good for it.

W. R. Johnson

Acknowledgments

I gratefully acknowledge and warmly thank Seth Schein and Elizabeth Horan for their meticulous criticism of all the translations. I am also indebted to Francis Dunn, and to Norman O. Brown, Helen Deutsch, Nancy Felson-Rubin, John Finamore, W. R. Johnson, Anthony Podlecki, Marilyn B. Skinner, and John Van Sickle for their helpful suggestions. The anonymous readers for the University of California Press, the editorial committee, and the editor, Doris Kretschmer, provided valuable assistance. I am grateful to my husband, David Hast, and my mother, Connie Rayor, for their skillful editing and steady encouragement.

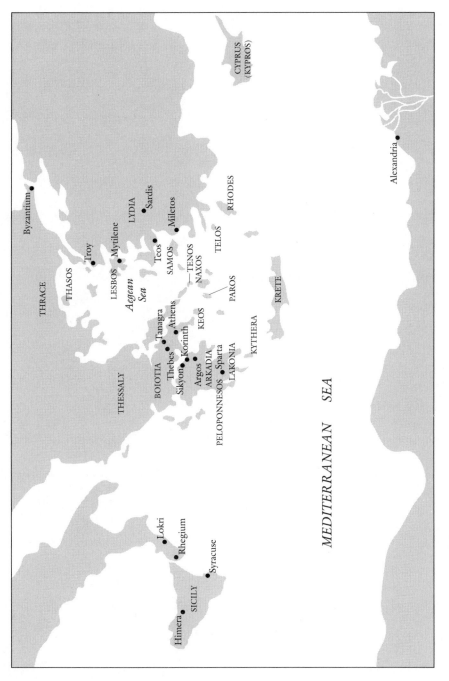

The world of the Greek poets

INTRODUCTION

Sappho's Lyre includes poets from the seventh to the second centuries B.C.E.: eight archaic lyric poets and nine later women poets. From the archaic period (the seventh and sixth centuries) Sappho is the only extant female poet, and is today the best known of all these poets. Three of the later women poets wrote in the fifth century, during the classical period when the great tragedies were produced in Athens. The remaining six women poets are from the Hellenistic period (dating from the death of Alexander the Great in 323 B.C.E. to 30 B.C.E.). This ancient poetry provides "glimpses that would make [us] less forlorn"[1]—glimpses into unfamiliar rituals and culture, somewhat familiar myths, and modern emotions. The poems speak of passion, friendship, betrayal, loss, and endurance. The unique voice of each poet draws us back in time and forward again in our recognition of its truth and beauty.

The first collection of Greek poetry was made in the third century B.C.E., at the royal court in Alexandria. After conquering Egypt, Alexander founded the city, which became the literary center of the Greek world. There Ptolemy II developed the impressive Museum and Library. Alexandrian scholars selected the work of nine lyric poets to preserve in editions and commentaries: Alkman, Stesichoros, Sappho, Alkaios, Ibykos, Anakreon,

1. William Wordsworth, "The World Is Too Much with Us."

1

Simonides, Bacchylides, and Pindar. This present anthology of Greek poetry includes poems by all but the last two. The extant poems of Pindar and Bacchylides are primarily epinikia, odes in praise of victors in the Panhellenic athletic games. Their work deserves a separate volume. *Sappho's Lyre* consists of a representative selection of the archaic lyric, beginning with the "father of lyric poetry," Archilochos, and includes the best-known poems, those in Campbell's (1967) Greek edition, the most recent papyrus finds, and personal favorites. All of Sappho's poems that are whole enough to make sense are included, as well as the complete surviving works of the later women writers Korinna, Praxilla, Telesilla, Erinna, Anyte, Nossis, Moiro, Hedyla, and Melinno.

I have gathered these particular poets together for reasons both pragmatic and poetic. There is no other single volume available that includes the complete women poets. Their poems are remarkable for their variety and appeal. As for the archaic lyric poets, I accept the Alexandrian canon, and exclude nonlyric poets of the archaic period for two reasons. First, the lyric poets composed their poems to be sung, accompanied by a lyre. The musical quality of these poems, in addition to their vivid and intriguing content, has always attracted modern readers. Their straightforward language and their use of sound make it imperative for us to translate these poems repeatedly into a modern lyric voice. Second, the nonlyric poetry from the same period is available elsewhere, and perhaps of more interest for its historical value than for the quality of the poetry itself.

These glimpses from the past are rarely complete because the seventeen poets collected here wrote a diversity of poetry now lost to us. No original manuscripts from the authors survive. Only a small quantity of poems remain from the large body of work, many with pieces missing. Indeed, of the nine books of Sappho's poetry collected in Hellenistic times (some five hundred poems), only one definitely complete poem remains.

The poetry survives only as quotations in other texts or in assorted papyri. Ancient grammarians interested in unusual meters, dialects, usage, or language quote whole poems occasionally, or more often lines or only a few words from poems. For example, a fragment of Alkman's poem 7 was quoted to show that he uses the word *knōdalon*, usually meaning any wild creature, to mean specifically a sea monster:

> All asleep: mountain peaks and chasms,
> ridges and cutting streams,
> the reptile tribes that black earth feeds,
> mountain beasts and race of bees,
> *monsters deep in the purple sea*,
> and tribes of long-winged birds all sleep.

Some notes on the poems, which can provide evidence for missing words, have been preserved in the margins of ancient manuscripts. These marginal notes, called scholia, are usually extracts from lengthier commentaries. The scholia on Alkman 1, for example, attest that the god Resource (*Poros*) was mentioned in the poem, although the word is now missing. In this instance, the scholium allows us to fill in a few vital missing words:

> . . . for Destiny [and Resource]
> . . . oldest of all [gods]

Since the works were copied by hand, however, there are frequent errors in the texts, especially in the placement of scholia.

Texts of all kinds were copied onto rolls of papyrus and stored in the library at Alexandria, among other places. Papyrus plants grew well along the Nile and were processed into a writing paper cheaper than parchment (animal skin) and more versatile for long works than carving in stone, painting on vases, or scratching into clay. The paper was made from strips of papyrus pith laid crosswise, soaked, and dried under pressure. Through the long intervening centuries, many papyrus manuscripts survived in the dry climate of Egypt. New discoveries continue to tantalize us. Unfortunately, Egyptian papyri containing poetry turn up in various stages of disintegration or in pieces. Old, worn papyrus rolls were reused in many ways. Like many other recent papyrus finds, Stesichoros 6 was found on strips of papyrus used to wrap a mummy. The poem as translated reflects the disintegration and tearing of the papyrus. Only the Hellenistic epigrams from the Greek Anthology, compiled around 100 B.C.E., have a relatively dependable manuscript tradition.

With the increased literacy and scholarly atmosphere of the Hellenistic period, poetry was written to be read. People read aloud to themselves or in small gatherings. We experience modern printed poetry in a similar fashion, although we generally read silently and privately. Archaic poetry, however, was written to be performed. Texts were copied primarily to assist in subsequent oral performances. The Alexandrian scholars in the third century were able to collect such a large selection of archaic poetry partly because it was popular enough to be performed (and therefore recopied) continuously throughout the centuries from the time of its composition until its compilation.[2]

Although we now consider Archilochos the father of lyric poetry, he is excluded from the Alexandrian list of lyric poets because his poetry, written in elegiac and iambic meters, was not sung. Elegiac (developed from epic hexameter) and iambic (considered the closest meter to regular speech by Aristotle and the meter of choice for invective poetry) were recited or chanted. The ancient term for lyric is "melic," from the Greek *melos*, meaning melody. Only poetry sung to a melody, therefore, was classified as lyric. Yet Archilochos presents the earliest example of poetry that today we would call lyric in theme and style. His poems primarily are brief and written in the first person about events and values of his society, as, for example, poem 3:

Some Thracian exults in an excellent shield,
which I left—not willingly—by a bush.
I saved myself. What do I care for that shield?
To hell with it. I'll buy one again, no worse.

2. See Herington for a complete discussion of performance and transmission of lyric poetry.

The difference between Archilochos and the lyric poets is less visible to us now because the music and spectacle of ancient lyric are gone. Yet the music *in* the poems, their lyric quality, has not faded with time.

Ancient lyric poetry contains a greater diversity of form and content than perhaps we would expect. Some of the once-sung poetry is like Archilochos', but there are also the long, mythological narratives of Stesichoros and Korinna, and the elaborate choral odes of Alkman.

Lyric poetry could be sung by a soloist or by a choir. Solo (monodic) lyric was considered more suitable for informal situations, and choral lyric for formal and ceremonial occasions. Both kinds of lyric were accompanied by musical instruments—usually a stringed instrument, either the lyre or a variety of lyre like the more elaborate *kithara* or lower-pitched *barbitos*, or, less commonly, a reed pipe (*aulos*). The poets themselves composed the melodic music, which enhanced the effects of the various Greek meters. The Greek language has an inherent melody in pitch accentuation and a quantitative meter based on long and short vowels. For monodic lyric, the singer accompanied himself or herself with the lyre at a small gathering of friends, such as a symposium (drinking party). Choral lyric included more instruments and the added element of dance. Under the direction of the poet, a chorus of seven to fifty men, women, boys, or girls, sang and danced at religious festivals, poetry competitions, and other citywide celebrations.

The performance conventions of choral lyric and monody provide us with clues to interpret the poetry. For example, although certain poems by Alkman and Sappho imply female homosexuality, their impact on an audience might have been quite different. The two poets use female same-sex attraction for different purposes, reflected in the different genres of choral and monodic lyric. In Alkman's partheneion, the homosexual attraction is part of a poem which seems to be encouraging marriage. In Sappho's poetry homoeroticism and marriage songs occur in separate poems.

Alkman 1 portrays female homosexuality in the context of a choral performance in a state-sponsored festival for a large, mixed-sex audience. The poem describes the attractions of the female chorus through their praise of each other, in order to present them as newly marriageable young women, appropriate objects of desire for men like the Spartan heroes listed in the fragmentary first part of the poem. Although the female chorus members seem to be conversing freely among themselves, we must remember that they sang and danced a rehearsed script. It would be inappropriate under the circumstances for Alkman to glorify female homosexuality in itself or to present the young women as objects of desire for women in the audience in this celebratory rite of transition. Sappho, on the other hand, probably sang most of her poems in small gatherings among a group of women friends. Under these circumstances Sappho could present erotic desire among women as a subject worthy of exploration in its own right.

The relationship of individuals to the community broadly distinguishes choral lyric from monody. Choral lyric supports the solidarity of the civic community through spectacular public productions. Choral hymns praise the gods, and praise humans as representatives of their city. With pithy statements on the relationship of humans to gods, choral lyric links mythic and contemporary events. In Alkman 1, aphorisms such as "Let no man fly to heaven . . . nor try to marry Aphrodite" connect the mythic tale of Spartan heroes defeated by the Dioscuri (Helen's brothers) to the contemporary performance, which praises the goddesses Aotis and Orthria (perhaps cult names for Helen or Aphrodite) and the choir itself. Lessons from the past thereby inform present values and the unity of the city.

Monodic lyric stresses the unity of a group with common interests as separate from other groups in the same city. Monody focuses on individual relationships—personal and political—concerning friendship, love, and betrayal. Using the conventions of praise and blame, the poetry praises group members and current friends and lovers, and vilifies members of other groups or former friends who switched alliances. A clear example of blame poetry would be Archilochos 9, which curses a former friend by wishing that, after being shipwrecked, he wash up naked on an enemy shore and be forced into slavery:

That I would like to see,
to him who wronged me and trampled his oaths,
who was my friend before.

Monody represents the personal voice of an individual (not necessarily that of the poet) within society; choral lyric represents the voice of a community.[3]

The poets did not necessarily restrict themselves to either choral lyric or monody alone. Furthermore, it is often difficult now to distinguish between the two forms. Although Stesichoros is usually classified as a choral poet, the epic content and narrative style of his poems suggest a solo singer. The remains of Sappho's, Alkaios', and Anakreon's poetry are primarily monodic, but at least Sappho's epithalamia were probably sung by a group. And the love poetry of the choral poets Alkman and Ibykos is probably monodic. Simonides was famous for his boys' choirs and choral victory odes, but much of his poetry translated here appears to be monodic.

The five earliest archaic poets performed locally; the later archaic poets travelled beyond their home territories. Ibykos provides the first examples of court poetry, written and performed not for a private circle of friends (as was the earlier monodic poetry) or by a citizen among citizens, but for the entertainment of a royal court. Ibykos, Anakreon, and Simonides each were invited to the court of a ruler, and supported by a patron of the arts. Poetry composed for the court tends toward lighter songs of drinking, love, and proverbs. A good example of proverbial poetry is Simonides 14, which may have been written for court symposia:

There is a tale
that Excellence lives on inaccessible rocks,
keeping to her holy place—
nor is she visible to the eyes of all
mortals, for whom heart-biting sweat

3. See Most (1982) for a detailed discussion of choral and monodic lyric.

does not come from within
and who do not reach that peak of prowess.

Simonides also is said to have been the first to write poetry for pay.

The location of the poet and the kind of lyric determines the poetic language used. Court poets, for example, do not necessarily use their home dialects, while poets such as Alkman, Sappho, and Alkaios, who write for their fellow citizens, do. In general, monody combines conventional language with vernacular in the local dialects of the poets, mostly Aeolic and Ionic (from the islands near Asia Minor). Choral song develops an artificial literary language highly influenced by the Doric dialect (from western and central Greece) regardless of each poet's own region. Of the choral poets, only Alkman uses his local dialect, which is the Lakonian (Spartan) version of Doric.

All the lyric poets use the diction of, and adapt formulas found in, the epic tradition. Formulas are the phrases, and even the whole scenes, repeated throughout epic poetry; they reflect the oral composition of epic. Although the earliest lyric poetry remaining today was written after Homer, lyric did not come after or develop from epic. Lyric has an oral tradition at least as old as epic's.[4] The advent of writing in the eighth century B.C.E. brought to a close the composition of oral epic and led to the first record of archaic lyric. (Fifth century Athenian drama combines both elements: the dialogue of epic with choral song.)

In language and in content the lyric poets often allude to epic, either to borrow the authority of tradition or to posit a contrasting ethic. Archilochos defines a practical heroic code in which honor is not bound to one's armor (poem 3) and appearance counts less than steadfastness in battle (poem 2):

I don't like a tall general, swaggering,
proud of his curls, with a fancy shave.
I'd rather have a short man, who looks
bow-legged, with a firm stride, full of heart.

4. See Nagy (1974) on the epic and lyric tradition.

In the *Iliad*, a man's appearance is expected to reflect his inner worth—Hektor's complaint against Paris is for having the looks without the substance.

Ibykos, a century later than Archilochos, mocks epic, only to call on it to provide "undying fame" (an epic formula) for his patron, Polykrates (poem 5, lines 47–48):

> And you, Polykrates, will have undying fame
> through song and my fame.

In his humorous "epic" poem, Ibykos speeds through the Trojan War like a two-minute *Hamlet*, only to say that epic is not his subject. He uses the epic frame to praise his patron: Polykrates will receive fame through Ibykos' poem, as did the Homeric heroes through epic.

The immediacy of the language leads us to read some lyric poems as if they were letters or windows into the poets' private lives. We need to remember that poets speak through various personae. The "I" of the speaker in a poem is not necessarily equivalent to the poet. Critics no longer tend to read a literary text, especially an ancient text, as a nonfiction record of the poet's life. Most of the so-called biographical information on the lives of ancient Greek poets has been shown to derive from later scholarly constructions based on the poetry itself.[5]

The controversy surrounding Archilochos 20, discovered in 1973, can help put biographical readings into perspective. The poem narrates a dialogue between the speaker and a woman, and her ensuing seduction. Archilochos combines the conventions of praise and blame poetry[6] in order to contrast two kinds of women, the one the narrator desires:

> I'd much rather have you
> because you are not faithless or two-faced,

5. See Lefkowitz.
6. See Nagy (1979).

and the one he rejects:

> Let another man
> have Neobule.
> No, she is over-ripe . . .

The biographical school of interpreters would consider that Archilochos, the man, describes a personal conquest and expresses personal hatred regarding two actual women. However, we should consider that Archilochos, the poet, uses a "lover persona" to narrate the story. This moves us away from speculation on the personal life of a poet dead for over twenty-five centuries, to the recognition of the distinction between the narrator and the author of a literary work. The poets tell stories through the various personae of their narrators.

The use of personae does not render the poetic voice somehow less direct or immediate. Lyric poetry was never a spontaneous outpouring of emotion; rather, it developed as a carefully crafted and stylized art from traditional literary conventions. Thus, when the speaker of Archilochos 3 refers to having lost his shield, whether the historical Archilochos actually did lose it is irrelevant. Sappho herself does not actually watch her beloved in conversation with a man as she recites her poem 8,

> that man has the fortune of gods,
> whoever sits beside you . . .

nor has Anakreon been slighted by a woman from Lesbos at the symposium where he sings (poem 4), "and she gapes after another girl." Trying to ferret out the "real" deed of an individual behind the poetic word leads one astray.

Biographical readings, or those based on the pretense that the audience merely overhears the poet's passionate expression of emotion, misjudge the purpose and ignore the context of lyric. For example, since Sappho describes human passions and situations in a deceptively simple manner, the passion in her poetry has been seen as the direct expression of a woman lacking self-control. In poem 8, Sappho skillfully combines an exploration of passion with a conventional formula of praise (like Odysseus' praise of the princess Nausikaa as he approaches her dirty and naked after being shipwrecked [*Odyssey* 6.145–69]).[7] The ancient poets did not speak to themselves or directly to the "you" in the poem, but to their audience. They composed with the audience in mind and for the purpose of performance. The poets use their own experiences to present ideas of the world, to persuade the audience to accept their view of reality. The lyric present, which is always now, draws the audience into the dramatic moment of the story.[8]

The fifth century women poets Korinna, Telesilla, and Praxilla continue the lyric tradition of the archaic poets, but lyric drops off sharply at the close of that century. From the late fourth and the third centuries Erinna, Anyte, Nossis, and Moiro wrote epigrams in elegiac couplets, and Moiro and Hedyla short mythical narratives in epic hexameters. Erinna also has a long lament in hexameters influenced by both Sappho and Homeric epic. In the second century Melinno returns to lyric with rather rigid Sapphic stanzas for her deification of Roman power.

Epigram, as opposed to the sung lyric, is a written, bookish form. The word "epigram" means "inscription." While epigrams began as actual inscriptions accompanying dedications or on tombstones, many or even most Hellenistic epigrams probably are purely literary. Their meter, elegiac couplets, emphasizes symmetry and closure (as if they were written on a tombstone). The literary pretense of epigrams is that they are inscribed on some sort of monument for passersby to read, as in poem 4 by Erinna:

> Stele and my sirens and mournful urn,
>   which holds the meagre ashes belonging to Hades,
> tell those passing by my tomb "farewell"
>   (be they townsmen or from other places)
> and that this grave holds me, a bride. Say too,

7. See Winkler (1981), 73–76.
8. See Johnson.

that my father called me Baukis and my family
is from Tenos, so they may know, and that my friend
Erinna on the tombstone engraved this epigram.

Epitaphs for unmarried or newly wed women or for warriors killed in battle, dedicatory epigrams, and "portrait" epigrams may have been written to stand on their own and may not refer to actual artifacts. Anyte, who probably invented the popular pastoral epigram and animal epitaphs, provides some evidence. Her insect and dolphin epitaphs certainly lead us to read all epigrams as potentially literary; for example, her poem 11:

No longer will I fling up my neck, exulting
in the buoyant seas arising from the deep,
nor around the ship's bow (with fine oarlocks)
do I blow, delighting in my figurehead:
the darkened seawater thrust me on land;
I lie beached by this shallow, sandy coast.

Some war-horses and prize dogs were given burial and tombstones, but it is hard to believe that all of the many animal epitaphs were actually inscribed on stone. A poet's fiction can include, of course, occasion as well as persona.

The archaic poets offered later poets a rich literary tradition, from love poems to mythological narratives. Some women's poetry clearly shows Sappho's influence, some is more like Stesichoros', and some is harder to pin down.

Sappho avoids either imitating or polemically rejecting the male literary tradition as she explores human values through women's experience. For example, in Greek poetry after Homer, Helen usually appears as the evil force whose lust for Paris causes the Trojan War (see Alkaios 5 and 6). Sappho, in poem 4, uses the myth to illustrate her argument that "whatever one loves" appears most desirable:

Some say an army of horsemen, others
say foot-soldiers, still others, a fleet,

is the fairest thing on the dark earth:
I say it is whatever one loves.

Sappho provides two examples: Helen illustrates the decision to follow what one loves, regardless of consequences or of whom one leaves behind. Anaktoria provides a contemporary example; the speaker remembers the absent Anaktoria, the fairest sight in her eyes. Sappho's poem does not judge or blame Helen for the consequences of her decision or reproach Anaktoria for her absence. Who is to blame for the destruction in the Trojan War, the woman who followed her desire for one man or the men who followed their desire for war? Sappho accepts Homer's position in the *Iliad*, that Helen should not be blamed for the war, but emphasizes Helen's choice and desire in the matter. The most beautiful woman, the object of men's desire, became the subject of desire in leaving her husband to follow her heart. Just as Helen preferred Paris over Menelaos, "the best man of all," so the speaker would rather see the absent Anaktoria than the traditionally male-valued glitter of war. Thus she presents a persuasive argument for her opening statement on desire: personal testimony is backed by the authority of the past (reinterpreted).

Besides Sappho, we know of no other women poets from the archaic period, with the possible exception of women mentioned in Sappho's and Alkman's poetry. Alkman says Megalostrata shows "this gift from the sweet Muses" (poem 6); perhaps she was a contemporary poet. Sappho mentions women who rival her in drawing young women into their circles. Andromeda attracts one of Sappho's young women: "you fly off to Andromeda" (poem 36). Poem 33 declares that an unnamed woman has "no part of the Pierian roses," that is, the art of poetry. These "rivals" may have been literary rivals, and the young women they attracted poets themselves. Yet only Sappho's work remains; there is no other direct evidence of women poets.

Perhaps Sappho's and Alkman's societies were more conducive to women writing than other places during the seventh and sixth centuries B.C.E. Women were active in public performances and contests in Sparta and

Lesbos; they seem to have had greater freedom of movement and association there. In addition, women of Sparta and Lesbos were reported as being sexually uninhibited. Alkman's and Sappho's poetry certainly provides evidence for the acceptance of female homoerotic relationships. Later sources, such as Plutarch, state that pedagogic homosexual relations among women were a normal part of Spartan society. In these settings, women may have had more opportunities, and recognition, for composing poetry.

More names of women poets survive from the fifth century, but only the fragmentary work of three. Perhaps other women wrote poetry for their home audiences (as Korinna, Telesilla, and Praxilla did), but their work was lost in time. Since few women travelled as performers, their writing would not have had the wide exposure of travelling male poets of the time. After the fifth century, in the Hellenistic period, we find many more female poets, perhaps due to better educational and travel opportunities for women than in earlier times.

One of the early Hellenistic writers, Erinna, looked back three centuries to Sappho for her inspiration. In her poem in epic hexameters, Erinna picks up Sappho's strong "I," her women-directed discourse, and borrows from her Aeolic dialect, but in a nonlyric form and meter. Erinna's poetry was meant to be read, not sung and performed as Sappho's was. Yet by focusing entirely on the life of one young woman and the death of her friend, presented in the first person singular, Erinna imitates the emotional immediacy of Sappho's lyric. Through Erinna's skillful use of personal content and epic meter, the poem reads both as a diary and a heroic (Iliadic) lament.[9]

Erinna writes about the loss of a beloved friend through the friend's marriage and subsequent death (poem 1):

> But when into the bed . . . you forgot everything
> that as a baby . . . you heard from your mother,
> dear Baukis; Aphrodite . . . forgetfulness.

9. See Skinner (1982).

She recalls the games of tag and dolls they played as children, and laments her death. Even in the fragmentary remains of her long poem, we can see the narrator's sense of loss at growing old without her friend. Her feelings are complicated by the fear of marriage, which led to her friend's death, as well as the desire not to remain in her mother's house unwed. In this poem Erinna explores women's fear of loneliness, marriage, death, and aging.

While Erinna recognizes Sappho as her literary foremother, other women poets made different choices. Korinna, for example, follows the more impersonal lyric tradition of mythological narrative, best exemplified by Stesichoros. Stesichoros does not seem to use myth to reflect on contemporary life, but for its own sake, putting epic tales to song. His long narratives present unusual versions of standard myths. He wrote two Helen poems, one of which reviles Helen, as Alkaios does, for deserting her husband (poem 2), and another, a palinode, which apologizes for the first poem. The palinode relates a different version of the events, as this fragment (poem 3) shows:

> This story is not true,
> you did not sail in full-decked ships
> nor reach the towers of Troy.

Stesichoros asserts that Helen never went to Troy; he may have originated the story that Zeus had Hermes carry Helen off to Egypt, while Paris took an image of her to Troy—Zeus used the Trojan war to combat overpopulation. According to legend, Stesichoros went blind after composing his first Helen poem and regained his vision after recanting in the second. Since the Spartans worshiped Helen as a goddess, the second version would please them better. His palinode inspired much art and Euripides' *Helen*.

Little is left of Stesichoros' Helen poems, but recently long papyrus fragments of two other unusual versions of myths, the Herakles and the Oedipus cycles (poems 5 and 6), have been found. One of Herakles' labors was to steal cattle from the three-bodied monster Geryon. In Stesichoros' story our sympathy is wholly for the monster. Geryon's mother begs him not to fight Herakles, and Geryon himself is reluctant. He doesn't know whether he inherited his father's immortality or his mother's mortality, but his sense of honor impels him to protect his cattle from the thieving Herakles (who is always supported by Zeus and Athena). He discovers the hard way that he takes after his mother.

The Oedipus papyrus shows a strong Jocasta proposing a way around the prophecy that her sons by Oedipus will either kill each other or destroy Thebes. Sophocles' Jocasta kills herself on discovering Oedipus' identity. Stesichoros' Jocasta not only survives the discovery, she later proposes a sensible way for her sons to divide Oedipus' inheritance: by lot, one will take the throne and rule, the other will keep the major possessions and leave town. Stesichoros' transformation of epic themes into lyric poetry provides a model for later writers.

Korinna's mythological narratives possess the odd slant, wry humor, and rich characterization found in Stesichoros' writing. Her poetry, however, is crafted particularly for a female audience. In one of her three long fragments (poem 1), Korinna emphasizes her poetic strategy and repertoire:

> Terpsichore [told] me
> lovely old tales to sing
> to the white-robed women of Tanagra,
> and the city delighted greatly
> in my voice, clear as the swallow's.

Korinna describes her art as reworking the old myths, "father-songs," in her own way to delight the women of her home town, Tanagra. This and other fragments show the poet's awareness of her double role in winning and conferring fame (*kleos*). Her popular poetry wins fame for her and for the subjects of her poetry. Like Ibykos in his poem written for Polykrates, she too celebrates her role in creating fame.

Korinna's narratives are about local heroes, both male and female, from her Boiotian district; she says, "I sing the excellence [*aretē*] of heroes, male and female" (poem 10). In the longer fragment, about a singing contest between the Boiotian mountains Kithairon and Helikon (poem 2), the winning song focuses on the goddess Rhea (rather than her son Zeus or husband Kronos). Rhea wins honor (*timē*) from the other gods when she tricks Kronos to save Zeus.

Hesiod composed the standard version of this story three hundrd years earlier. His *Theogony* describes the transition of power from female to male: from Gaia (Mother Earth) who gives virgin birth to her husband, to her grandson Zeus who gives solo birth to Athena. Kronos and Zeus each gain power through conquering their fathers; Zeus keeps his power by preventing his wife from conceiving the son that would conquer him (he swallows her). Korinna takes one part of Hesiod's story and reworks it for her audience of women. She changes the tale of Rhea and Kronos by putting it in another context (from succession story to singing contest) and by emphasizing Rhea's heroic action. In Korinna's poem Rhea is the heroine, the clever woman who saves her son by outwitting his crafty father. In a society in which the father decided whether to let a newborn baby live or die through exposure, this story must have touched a chord with the female audience—a mother, seen in a heroic manner, able to save her child, regaining control over her progeny, and winning honor for doing so.

Korinna's poem continues with the results of the contest. The gods vote on the two songs and crown Kithairon the victor. Helikon is a poor loser, throwing a temper tantrum in which he rips out large chunks of a mountain. Korinna thus repossesses tradition without breaking from it. She places a familiar story in an unusual framework.

The ancient poets draw on their expansive poetic tradition and add their unique voices. Poems that have survived through the ages provide a glimpse of the past mingled with the present through these translations—a new blend of tradition and innovation. These voices from the past join us in our own modern poetic voice.

▼   ▼   ▼

A translation and its Greek text depend on each other to live. New translations become necessary because perceptions of texts and culture, literary and translation theory, and language and styles of poetry change over time. In the past, translators have had a tendency to add or subtract phrases, and have sometimes used poor texts not based on the latest findings or the most accurate scholarship. Assumptions concerning ancient poetry, and especially women's poetry, have sometimes contributed to distorted or censored renderings. Obvious examples include translations that switch pronouns or even the subject from female to male. And some translations fill in the fragment gaps with inappropriate or trivializing phrases.

Reading a translation should be as close to the experience of reading the Greek text as possible. The reader, however, can only discover the possibilities of the Greek text through the eyes of the translator. One language cannot be copied into another language intact, as if through tracing paper. The poem enters and exits the translator, filtered through individual bias and insight. A translator is the most active of readers—reading, interpreting, and then writing that interpretation into a new text for new readers.

Each translation is crafted from a multitude of decisions concerning the relative importance of different aspects of the Greek text. Thus the translation expresses whatever the translator perceives as most important. For example, in a prose translation of poetry, the translator has decided that form and content can be separated, that it is enough to record content. Although the "soul of sweet delight can never be defil'd",[10] if the poetry is lost in the transfer, so is the poem.

Through specific choice of words and style, the translations here reflect my individual response to the ancient poetry. My response is informed by knowledge of Greek and of the historical context of the poetry. My gender, my background in contemporary American culture, and my personal enjoyment of contemporary American poetry also influence that response. To-

10. William Blake, *The Marriage of Heaven and Hell*.

gether, the cultural context of translator and text define the kinds of translations that are possible at any given time.

In translating this poetry, I decided to respond to poetry with poetry (not prose), to use our modern poetic idiom (instead of archaizing), to keep the ancient images (not substitute modern ones), to recreate sound and tempo effects where possible (but not meter), not to impose formal rhyme schemes on unrhymed poetry, and to show the fragmentary state of our texts (not pretend they are whole). I tried to retain specific details, while compensating for formal aspects that work clumsily in English, such as meter, to recreate the vivid and direct effects of the Greek.

In translating fragments, the gaps need to be represented along with the words. Fragments force readers to read between the lines, to draw mental connections between gaps. It is the task of the translator to make this extra reading effort worthwhile, but without providing the words she imagines might have been there.

It has sometimes been fashionable to expand, sometimes to trim the text translated. Overtranslation and undertranslation erase evidence of physical gaps in fragmentary texts. "Completing" the poem by filling in gaps overly privileges the translator's interpretation, and fragmentary lines left out through condensing often contain vital information. Both practices simplify the poetry and mislead the reader. While the translator's interpretation of the text always informs the translation, she should resist the temptation to add or subtract text itself.

The standard Greek editions include generally accepted supplements based on quotations in other ancient authors, probable readings of papyri, information from scholia, and the sense of the texts themselves. The translator accepts or rejects these supplements on an individual basis according to probability and necessity. It is not overtranslation to accept a suggested word that is likely paleographically and needed for an intelligible reading. For example, in Archilochos 20, line 52, one editor, Page (1974), supplies the adjective "white": "I released my white force." Since the line almost certainly refers to the ejaculation of semen, "white" is a necessary clarification of "force." Some additions to fragmented texts are acceptable, and it would be a disservice not to include them.

On the other hand, early editions of the Greek, such as Edmonds' Sappho (1928), contain large-scale reconstruction. Edmonds fills in passages missing in the extant texts of Sappho; he even composes entire poems from a few fragments. More recent editions of Sappho by Lobel and Page (1955) and Voigt (1971) provide texts free from these restorations. Translations based on poorer editions, therefore, are an additional stage removed from the original poetry.

The translator can make the most of the extant text by indicating missing parts through line breaks and punctuation. Some translations can even imitate the physical texture of the papyrus by showing where the lines were torn (see the beginning of Alkman 1). My translations provide the typographical signs of absence and uncertainty that least hinder reading: an asterisk to mark a missing line, ellipsis dots for missing words, and an occasional bracket to enclose words illegible in the text, but fairly certain and necessary to the sense:

. . .	word or words missing
*	line missing
* * *	many lines missing
[ ]	highly likely reading, often partially legible in manuscript
( )	paraphrase from other sources or educated guess
§§	beginning or ending of poem is certain

The translations are grouped by poet in the probable chronological order of the poets' lives. The selections from each poet are thematically arranged where possible. Each poet's poems are numbered sequentially in the body of the text; the notes provide the numeration of the Greek editions.

ARCHILOCHOS

1

I am a servant of the War Lord
and of the Muses, knowing their desirable gift.

2

I don't like a tall general, swaggering,
proud of his curls, with a fancy shave.
I'd rather have a short man, who looks
bow-legged, with a firm stride, full of heart.

3

Some Thracian exults in an excellent shield,
which I left—not willingly—by a bush.
I saved myself. What do I care for that shield?
To hell with it. I'll buy one again, no worse.

4

Heart, my heart churning with fathomless cares,
Get up! Fight! Heave your chest against the foe,
standing firm near the enemy's shafts.
And don't exult openly in victory,
5 nor in defeat collapse at home and weep.
But rejoice in joys and chafe at evils—
not too much. Recognize what rhythm holds men.

5

Attribute all to the gods: often they raise
up out of evils men who lie on the dark earth,
but often they knock flat on their backs
men who walk tall. Then many evils are born,
and one wanders without sustenance or wits.

6

No townsman, Perikles, will blame us for groaning
with cares, nor will the city celebrate feasts:
Such men the waves of the thundering sea
washed under, that our lungs are swollen
5 with sorrow. But for incurable ills, my friend,
the gods created powerful endurance
as a drug. Pain strikes one, then another.
Now it turns to us and we groan over a bloody
wound; next it'll turn to someone else. So now
10 endure, driving back womanly grief.

7

§§ Nothing is unexpected or sworn impossible,
nothing is amazing since Olympian Father Zeus
made night out of high noon, hiding the light
of the blazing sun; and damp fear came upon men.
5 Since then all things are credible and expected
by men: Let nothing you see amaze you even if
animals take the place of dolphins in their salty
pasture, and love the echoing waves of the sea
more than dry land, while dolphins take to the wooded hills.
10   . . . son of Archenax
                . . . child . . .
            . . . marriage . . .

8

§§ Glaukos, look: already the deep sea is troubled
     with waves, around Gyrai's heights a cloud stands upright,
     a sign of storm, and fear takes hold from the unexpected.

9

     . . . buffeted by the waves,
     and in Salmydessos may barbaric Thracians
     [most] gladly seize him
     naked—then he will have his fill of evils
5   eating the bread of slavery!—
     stiff with cold, and after the briny foam
     may thick seaweed cover him, and may he
     chatter his teeth, like a helpless dog
     lying mouth down at the very
10 edge of the breaking surf . . .
     That I would like to see,
     to him who wronged me and trampled his oaths,
     who was my friend before.   §§

10

§§ "What Gyges so golden has doesn't matter to me,
     envy never yet seized me, I'm not jealous
     of the gods' work, nor do I lust for high tyranny:
     these things are far from my eyes."

11

Here is a fable men tell,
how the fox and the eagle once mingled
in partnership.

12

You see that high crag,
jagged and malignant?
There he sits, scorning your battle-strength.

13

Zeus, Father Zeus, you've power over heaven,
you oversee the deeds, wicked and
lawful, of men, and you care about
the violence and justice of beasts.

14

The fox knows many things;
the hedgehog, one big thing.

15

She delighted to hold a slip of myrtle
and flowering rose;
                        her hair
shaded her shoulders and back.

16

Miserable I lie in desire,
lifeless, with bitter pains from the gods
pierced through my bones.

17

Such passion for love coiled in my heart
poured a thick mist over my eyes,
after stealing from my breast the tender senses.

18

If only I might touch Neobule's hand.

19

My friend, limb-loosening
desire conquers me.

20

". . . hold back completely;
equally endure . . .

but if you urge on and passion drives you,
there's a woman in our house
5   who now deeply desires . . .

a lovely, delicate woman—I think her
figure has no flaw—
you may make her . . ."

After she said that, I replied:
10 "Daughter of Amphimedo,
who was a noble and wise

woman, now buried in the dank earth,
there are many delights
of the goddess for young men

15 aside from the divine thing: one will do.
But at our leisure
when it grows dark . . .

you and I will make our plans, god willing.
I shall do as you say;
20   much . . .

but beneath the cornice and gates . . .
Don't refuse me, dear—
I'll hold to the garden grass,

you can count on it. Let another man
25   have Neobule.
No, she is over-ripe . . .

her virgin bloom has flowed away
and her former charm.
She couldn't get her fill—

30   the mad woman showed her measure of . . .
To hell with her!
May this not . . .

that I, keeping such a woman,
will be the neighbors' joke.
35   I'd much rather have you

because you are not faithless or two-faced,
while she is much keener
and makes many men . . .

I fear that urging on in haste I may breed
40   blind and untimely things,
like the bitch's litter."

I said such things, and taking the girl
I laid her down, wrapped
in a soft cloak, in the blooming

45 flowers, my arms embracing her neck;
she was [still] with fear
like a fawn . . .

and I gently took her breasts in my hands,
. . . her fresh skin showed
50 the bloom of youth,

and caressing all her lovely body
I released my white force,
just touching her golden hair.   §§

ALKMAN

1

     . . . Polydeukes.
    . . . I don't count Lykaithos among the dead
   . . . but Enarsphoros and swiftfooted Sebros
       . . . the forceful . . .
5   . . . the warrior,
and Euteiches and lord Areitos
      . . . and . . . outstanding among demigods,

       . . . the hunter
      . . . great, and Eurytos
10   . . . tumult
      . . . and . . . the best men
      . . . we shall pass over.
      . . . for Destiny [and Resource]
      . . . oldest of all [gods]
15   . . . unshod strength . . .
Let no man fly to heaven
      . . . nor try to marry Aphrodite
      . . . queen or some

                    . . . or a daughter of Porkos,
20   . . . but the Graces with looks of love
                    . . . the house of Zeus.

      *

                    . . . a god
                    . . . to friends
25   . . . gave gifts
      *

                    . . . youth perished

      *

      *

30   . . . went: one of them by an arrow
                    . . . another by a marble millstone
                    . . . Hades

      *

                    . . . they suffered unforgettably
35   after contriving evil deeds—

      there is a vengeance of the gods—
      but he is blessed, who with wisdom
      weaves his day to the end
      without tears. And I sing
40   of Agido's radiance: I see
      her as the sun, which Agido
      calls as witness to shine
      for us. Yet for me either to praise
      or blame her, the glorious chorus leader
45   in no way allows, but she herself
      stands out just as if someone
      should set among the herds a horse,

sturdy, prize-winning, thunderhoofed,
from dreams beneath the rock.

50 Don't you see? The racer
is Enetic, but the hair
of my cousin
Hagesichora blooms
like pure gold,
55 and her silver face—
why should I tell you clearly?
Here is Hagesichora,
but the second after Agido in beauty
will run as a Kolaxaian horse with an Ibenian:
60 for these Peleiades, rising through ambrosial
night like the star Sirius,
while we bring the robe to Orthria,
fight with us.

Neither could such an abundance
65 of purple exist as to defend us,
nor an intricate snake
all gold, nor Lydian
hairband, the delight
of dark-eyed girls,
70 not Nanno's hair,
nor even divine Areta,
not Sylakis and Kleisisera;
nor once at Ainesimbrota's will you say:
Oh that Astaphis be mine,
75 may Philylla look over
and Damareta and desired Ianthemis—
but Hagesichora overwhelms me.

For isn't lovely-ankled
Hagesichora here?
80 She remains beside Agido
and praises our feasts.
O gods, receive their [prayers]:
from the gods come success
and fulfillment. Chorusleader,
85 I would speak—myself a girl
screeching in vain, an owl
from a rafter—still I want most
to please Aotis, since she has been
the healer of our toils;
90 but through Hagesichora young women
enter into desired peace.

For . . . by the trace-horse
*
and on a ship one must
95 listen above all to the navigator.
Yet she is [not] more musical
than the Sirens:
they are goddesses, but instead of eleven
these ten girls sing;
100 she sings like a swan on the streams
of Xanthos. The one with alluring golden hair
*
*
*
105 *   §§

2

Olympian [Muses], round my mind
       . . . of song, I
       . . . to hear
       . . . voice
5   . . . singing a beautiful song
    *

will scatter sweet sleep from my eyelids,
    . . . and leads me to join the contest
where I most of all will shake my golden hair.

10   . . . soft feet
* * *
61 with limb-loosening desire, but more meltingly
than sleep or death she glances over—
nor in vain sweet . . .

Astymeloisa doesn't answer me,
65 but holding the garland
like a star
falling through the radiant sky
or a golden branch or soft feather
    *
70   . . . she walked by on slender feet;
          . . . moist grace of Kinyras
          . . . sits on the virgins' hair.

          . . . Astymeloisa among the assembly
          . . . object of care to the people
75   . . . she took
          . . . I say:

. . . would that she toss a silver cup
. . . I could see if somehow
. . . she might love me,
80 coming near she might take my soft hand—
at once I would become her suppliant.

But now . . . a thoughtful girl
                    . . . holding me
                    . . . the girl
85   . . . grace

3

No longer, O honeytongued, holyvoiced maidens,
can my limbs carry me. How I wish I were a kingfisher
who flies above the blossoming foam with halcyons,
fearless-hearted, a holy sea-purple bird.

4

But often on the mountain peaks when
the festival with many torches pleases
the gods, holding a golden vessel,
a great bowl, such as shepherd men have,
5 pouring milk of a lioness in by hand
you made a great whole cheese
for the slayer of Argos.

5

It isn't Aphrodite, but wild Eros
plays like a boy,
going down on the touch-me-not
flower tips of galingale.

6

Love, again sweetly streaming down
from the Kyprian, warms my heart.

Goldenhaired Megalostrata,
blessed maiden, showed this
gift from the sweet Muses.

7

All asleep: mountain peaks and chasms,
ridges and cutting streams,
the reptile tribes that black earth feeds,
mountain beasts and race of bees,
5   monsters deep in the purple sea,
and tribes of long-winged birds all sleep.

STESICHOROS

1

They flung many quinces toward the chariot
for the king, and also many myrtle leaves,
and rose garlands and twined wreaths of violet.

2

        . . . since Tyndareos
sacrificing once to all the gods forgot only
generous Aphrodite; and she, in her anger, made
the daughters of Tyndareos twice wed and thrice wed
and husband deserters.

3

This story is not true,
you did not sail in full-decked ships
nor reach the towers of Troy.

4

(a) . . . Helen suddenly saw a divine omen
and so she spoke up to the son of Odysseus:
"Telemachos, whoever this messenger is from the sky
who vaulted down to us through the barren air,

5   . . . screaming with blood-red . . .
[Odysseus] appearing at your house
                . . . man
                . . . by the counsels of Athena
                . . . screeching crow herself

10   . . . nor will I detain you
. . . Penelope, on seeing you, son of a dear father,
                        . . . good
                        . . . divine . . .

(b) a silver . . .
with gold on top . . .
from Troy . . .
the son of Pleisthenes . . .

5 and some things . . .
        *
golden . . .

5

(i. The birthplace of Eurytion, Geryon's herdsman whom Herakles kills.)

Across from glorious Erytheia,
by the boundless, silver-rooted springs
of the Tartessos river, [she bore him]
in a rocky hollow.

(ii. Eurytion, as a child, and his mother leave Tartessos.)

Through waves of the deep sea,
they reached the gods' beautiful island,
where the Hesperides have their homes
all of gold.

(iii. Another herdsman tells Geryon about Herakles' murder of Eurytion.)

"of painful . . .
But my friend, your mother Kallirhoa
and Chrysaor, dear to Ares, . . ."

(iv. Geryon determines to fight Herakles to try to regain his cattle.)

with his hands . . .
and answering him
spoke the strong son
of immortal Chrysaor and Kallirhoa:
5   "Don't try to scare my manly heart
by bringing up chill death,
and do not . . . me . . .
If I am immortal in race
and unaging, and so will share
10   in life on Olympos,

better . . .
disgrace . . .

and . . .
horned . . .
15 of our . . .
But if, my friend, I must
reach hateful old age,
and live among ephemeral men
apart from the blessed gods,
20 now it is much more noble for me to suffer
whatever is destined . . .

and reproaches . . .
and on the whole race . . .
the son of Chrysaor in the future.
25 May this not be dear
to the blessed gods.
         . . . concerning my cattle
    *

      . . . glory . . ."

(v. Geryon's mother implores him not to fight Herakles.)

      . . . keeping watch . . .
and she saw that he would come . . .

victory . . . power . . .
hated . . .
5   . . . white . . .
Obey, my son . . .
  *
  *
Aegis-bearing . . .
10 great . . .
  *

no longer . . .
death . . .
but . . .
15 *
  *
by hand . . .

(vi. His mother continues her entreaty.)

" . . . I who am unhappy and cursed in giving birth
and in my suffering accursed things,
. . . Geryon, I implore you,
if ever I held out my breast to you

5   ✳

     ✳

by your dear mother brightening
        . . . with glad thoughts."

        . . . fragrant dress . . .

(vii. At the council of the gods, Athena asks Poseidon not to save Geryon.)

. . . stay beside Zeus,
ruler of all . . .

Then shining-eyed Athena
spoke eloquently to her strong-
5   minded uncle, driver of horses:
"Come, remembering the promise
which you undertook
        . . . Geryon from death . . ."

(viii. Herakles kills Geryon by stealth.)

(a)   . . . Herakles divided his thoughts

    *

       . . . to be much more profitable
       . . . to fight by stealth

5   . . . powerful
       . . . he planned for him
       . . . bitter death.
       . . . Geryon held his shield in front

    *

10   . . . from his head

    *

       . . . the helmet decked with horse hair,
       . . . on the ground . . .

(b)   . . . of hateful
death . . .
having . . . around its head,
defiled with blood . . . and with . . . bile,

5 with agonies from the mankilling,
gleaming-necked Hydra: in silence,
it treacherously pressed into his forehead
and split flesh and bones
by a god's dispensation.
10 The arrow held straight through
to the top of his head
and then fouled with dark-red blood
the breastplate and his goried limbs;

then Geryon bent his neck
15   at an angle, as when a poppy,
       dishonoring its delicate body,
       suddenly sheds its petals . . .

(ix. Herakles hits Geryon's second head with his club?)

His second . . .
club . . .

(x. After Herakles returns the giant bowl to the Sun, he takes the cattle to Tiryns.)

When the son of Hyperion
went down into the golden bowl
so that once across the holy ocean
he might come to the depths
5   of black night,
to his mother and wedded wife
and dear children,
the son of Zeus went on foot
into a grove shaded with bay trees . . .

(xi. Herakles has a drink with the centaur Pholos.)

Taking the rough bowl of three bottles' measure,
holding it up he drank, the bowl Pholos
had mixed and set beside him.

6

"Don't pile cruel cares upon those griefs
nor later predict for me
unbearable fears.

Not always equally
5   do the immortal gods set constant strife
on the holy earth for mortals,
nor indeed love; the gods set
[men's minds a day at a time].
May lord Apollo, the far-shooter,
10 not fulfill all your prophecies.

But if to see my children killed by each other
is my destiny that the Fates have spun,
let the fulfillment of hated death come for me now
before I ever see these things,
15 with griefs full of groans and tears . . .
my children in the palace
dead or the city sacked.

But come, children, [obey] my words, dear boys—
I am predicting for you fulfillment in this way:
20 that one keep the house and live [in Thebes]
and that the other leave with the cattle
and all the gold of his dear father,
whoever by lot first shakes out
a portion by the will of the Fates.

25 This, I think,
might be a way out for you from evil destiny

in accordance with the divine prophet's warnings,
if the son of Kronos [might protect]
the new generation and the city of lord Kadmos,
30 putting off for a long time the evil things [for Thebes]
that have been fated to happen."

So said the divine woman, speaking with gentle words
to stop the children from strife in the palace,
with mantic Teiresias in accord, and they obeyed
35 *

                                    . . . Theban
land . . .
     *

                        . . . and keeping precious gold
40 *

                        . . . they apportioned the glorious flocks
     *

                        . . . horses
     *
45 *

     *

                        . . . obscure
     *

                        . . . in their breast
50 *

                        . . . and he himself jumped up
     *

                        . . . he made a speech
     *

```
                    . . . a plan
       *
                    . . . having persuaded
       *
59     *


                    . . . many things for you both
       * * *
                    . . . having set up great . . .
     [Argos] . . .
                    . . . curve-horned cattle and horses
                    . . . portion

                    . . . which is destined . . .
75                  . . . of the king, Adrastos,
                    . . . who will give you his lovely daughter
       *
                    . . . the people will give
       *
80                  . . . of the king

                    . . . Eteokles continually . . .
                    . . . terribly in his breast
                    . . . to have Polyneikes'
       *
85   he will cause [ruin] for the whole city
       *
     forever . . . sorrow


       *
     especially . . . of all the gods
90     *
```

So said renowned Teiresias, and immediately . . .
home . . .
he went . . . for dear Polyneikes . . .
Thebes . . .

95   . . . he walked to the great wall
                              . . . for him
many . . .
men . . .
escorts . . . and they came to the Isthmos
100   sea . . .
                              . . . [with prayers]

                    . . . the lovely city of Korinth
and swiftly set out for pleasant Kleonai . . .

SAPPHO

1

§§ On the throne of many hues, Immortal Aphrodite,
child of Zeus, weaving wiles—I beg you
not to subdue my spirit, Queen,
with pain or sorrow

5 but come—if ever before
having heard my voice from far away
you listened, and leaving your father's
golden home you came

in your chariot yoked with swift, lovely
10 sparrows bringing you over the dark earth
thick-feathered wings swirling down
from the sky through mid-air

arriving quickly—you, Blessed One,
with a smile on your unaging face
15 asking again what have I suffered
and why am I calling again

and in my wild heart what did I most wish
to happen to me: "Again whom must I persuade
back into the harness of your love?
20 Sappho, who wrongs you?

For if she flees, soon she'll pursue,
she doesn't accept gifts, but she'll give,
if not now loving, soon she'll love
even against her will."

25 Come to me now again, release me from
this pain, everything my spirit longs
to have fulfilled, fulfill, and you
be my ally.   §§

2

Come to me from Krete to this holy
temple, to the apple grove,
the altars smoking
with frankincense,

5   cold water ripples through apple
branches, the whole place shadowed
in roses, from the murmuring leaves
deep sleep descends,

where horses graze, the meadow blooms
10 spring flowers, the winds
breathe softly . . .
    *

Here, Kypris, after gathering . . . ,
pour into golden cups
15 nectar lavishly
mingled with joys.

3

§§ Queen Hera, may your [graceful form]
   . . . near me—
   the prayer of the Atreidai . . .
   kings;

5 after accomplishing . . .
   first around [Troy] . . .
   they departed to this land,
   but could not . . .

   until . . . you and Zeus . . .
10 and Thyone's alluring [son].
   Now . . .
   as in [olden times].

   Holy and . . .
   [virgin] . . .

4

§§ Some say an army of horsemen, others
say foot-soldiers, still others, a fleet,
is the fairest thing on the dark earth:
I say it is whatever one loves.

5 Everyone can understand this—
consider that Helen, far surpassing
the beauty of mortals, leaving behind
the best man of all,

sailed away to Troy. She had no
10 memory of her child or dear parents,
since she was led astray
[by Kypris] . . .

*

         . . . lightly
15 . . . reminding me now of Anaktoria
being gone,

I would rather see her lovely step
and the radiant sparkle of her face
than all the war-chariots in Lydia
20 and soldiers battling in shining bronze.

5

And you, Dika, put lovely garlands round your hair,
weaving together slips of anise with gentle hands:
since the blessed Graces look more to the flowerful,
but turn away from the ones without garlands.

6

A many-colored sandal
covered her feet,
fine Lydian work.

7

The stars around the fair moon
hide away their radiant form
whenever in fullness she lights
the earth . . .

8

§§ To me it seems
    that man has the fortune of gods,
    whoever sits beside you, and close,
    who listens to you sweetly speaking
5 and laughing temptingly;
    my heart flutters in my breast,
    whenever I look quickly, for a moment—
    I say nothing, my tongue broken,
    a delicate fire runs under my skin,
10 my eyes see nothing, my ears roar,
    cold sweat rushes down me,
    trembling seizes me,
    I am greener than grass,
    to myself I seem
15 needing but little to die.

    But all must be endured, since . . .

9

     . . . I urge you . . .
       . . . taking . . .
the lyre, while desire again . . .
wings round you

5   beautiful one, since the dress . . .
you saw excited you, and I rejoice
because the Kyprian herself
once blamed . . .

so I pray . . .
10   this . . .
I want . . .

10

    . . . of love . . .
*

    . . . I look on you facing (me) . . .
      . . . as Hermione . . .
5 . . . but to liken you to goldenhaired Helen
*

. . . mortal women, but know that these . . . by your
. . . would . . . all my thought

*

10 *

               . . . [dewy] banks

*

       . . . to celebrate all night long.

11

May I, goldencrowned Aphrodite,
cast this lot . . .

12

I think no woman of such skill
will see the light of day ever again.

13

For you beautiful ones my mind
is unchangeable.

14

"I simply wish to die."
Weeping she left me
and said this too:
"We've suffered terribly
5   Sappho I leave you against my will."
I answered, go happily
and remember me,
you know how we cared for you,
if not, let me remind you
10   . . . the lovely times we shared.

Many crowns of violets,
roses and crocuses
. . . together you set before me
and many scented wreaths
15   made from blossoms
around your soft throat . . .
. . . with pure, sweet oil
. . . you anointed me,
and on a soft, gentle bed . . .
20   you quenched your desire . . .
. . . no holy site . . .
we left uncovered,
no grove . . . dance
. . . sound

15

. . . Sardis . . .
often holding her [thoughts] here

*

you, like a goddess undisguised,
5   but she rejoiced especially in your song.

Now she stands out among
Lydian women as after sunset
the rose-fingered moon

exceeds all stars; light
10   reaches equally over the brine sea
and thick-flowering fields,

a beautiful dew has poured down,
roses bloom, tender parsley
and blossoming honey clover.

15   Pacing far away, she remembers
gentle Atthis with desire,
perhaps . . . consumes her delicate soul;

to go there . . . this not
knowing . . . much
20   she sings . . . in the middle.

It is not easy for us to rival
the beautiful form of goddesses,
. . . you might have . . .

25　*

And . . . Aphrodite

　　　　　　. . . poured nectar from
a golden . . .
. . . with her hands Persuasion . . .

16

§§　Once again that loosener of limbs, Love,
bittersweet and inescapable, crawling thing,
seizes me.

17

Gongyla . . .

Surely a sign . . .
especially . . .
[Hermes] came into . . .

5　I said: O Lord . . .
By the blessed [goddess]
I take no pleasure on [earth]

but longing to die holds me,
to see the dewy lotus-
10　shaded banks of Acheron . . .

18

§§ Sweet mother, I cannot weave—
slender Aphrodite has overwhelmed me
with longing for a boy.

19

Love shook my senses,
like wind crashing on mountain oaks.

20

For me neither honey nor bee . . .

21

I don't expect to touch heaven . . .

22

[Eros] came from heaven wearing a purple cloak.

23

They say that once Leda found
an egg hidden in the hyacinth.

24

You came and did (well); I felt for you
and you cooled my spirit burning with desire.

25

May you sleep on the breast of a tender companion.

26

§§ Black Dream, you come . . .
and when sleep . . .

Sweet god, wonderfully from sorrow . . .
to keep separate the power . . .

5 and I hope I will not share . . .
nothing of the blessed . . .

for I would not be so . . .
delights . . .

and may I have . . .
10 them all . . .   §§

27

§§ The moon and Pleiades have set
half the night is gone
time passes
I sleep alone . . .

28

But as my friend, take to a younger bed;
I won't endure living with you, since I'm the elder.

29

            . . . you
. . . put success in the mouth

      . . . beautiful gifts, children
      . . . song-lover . . . from high, sweet lyres

5   . . . old age already . . . all skin
       . . . and hairs [turned] from black to [white]

        . . . and knees do not bear
       . . . like fawns

         . . . but what should I do?
10   . . . impossible to be . . .

          . . . rosy-armed Dawn
         . . . taking (Tithonos) to the ends of earth

           . . . nevertheless (old age) seized (him)
          . . . wife

15   . . . believes
           . . . might grant

But I love luxuriance, . . . this, and passion for the light
of life has granted me splendor and beauty.   §§

30

Their souls became cold
and their wings fell slack.

31

beneath its wings
pours out a shrill song,
when flying over the blazing
[earth it trills aloud].

32

Superior, as a singer from Lesbos to those of other lands.

33

When you die you'll lie dead, no memory of you
no [desire] will survive since you've no part
of the Pierian roses. But once gone,
you'll flutter among the obscure,
invisible still in the house of Hades.

34

What country woman bewitches your mind . . .
wrapped in country clothes . . .
not knowing how to draw her skirts around her ankles?

35

§§ I loved you Atthis once long ago . . .
You seemed to me a small child and without charm.

36

Atthis, for you the thought of me has become hateful,
and you fly off to Andromeda.

37

. . . Mika
. . . but I will not allow you
. . . you chose the friendship of Penthilian women
. . . malignant, our . . .
5   . . . sweet song . . .
. . . soft voice . . .
. . . and high, clear-sounding . . .
. . . dewy . . .

38

       . . . Kypris,
may she find you very bitter
and may Doricha not boast, saying
how she came the second time
to longed-for love.

39

When anger spreads in the breast,
guard against an idly barking tongue.

40

May winds and sorrows
carry him away who condemns . . .

41

A handsome man is good to look at,
but a good man will be handsome as well.

42

I wish to say something to you, but shame
prevents me . . .

43

But I am not someone of spiteful
temper—I have a gentle spirit.

44

§§ Kypris and Nereids, let that brother
    of mine come here unharmed
    and all that his heart desires
    be fulfilled,

5   may he release all past mistakes
    and to his friends be a joy,
    [a pain] to enemies—may no one again
    [be trouble] for us,

    may he desire to endow his sister
10 with honor, but in painful troubles
                . . . grieving before . . .
    *

                . . . hearing . . . a millet seed
                . . . of the citizens . . .
15 *
    *

    *
                . . . and you, Kypris
                . . . putting aside, from evils . . .
20 *   §§

45

§§ I have a beautiful child, her form
like golden flowers, beloved Kleis
whom I would not trade for all of Lydia
or lovely . . .

46

(a)   . . . My mother . . .

in her youth it was a great
adornment if someone had her hair
wrapped round with a purple [braid,]

5   it really was.
But for the one with hair
more golden than a pinetorch

. . . fitted with garlands
of blooming flowers.
10   Recently a hairband of many hues

from Sardis . . .
          . . . cities . . .

(b)   But for you, Kleis, I have no colorful
hairband—where will it come from?—
but the Mytilenean . . .

      *

5   *
              . . . many-hued . . .

these keepsakes of exile . . .
Kleanax's sons . . .
These have wasted away terribly . . .

47

Evening Star who gathers everything
shining dawn scattered—
you bring the sheep and the goats,
you bring the child back to its mother.

48

The sweet apple reddens on a high branch
high upon highest, missed by the applepickers:
no, they didn't miss, so much as couldn't touch.

49

Herdsmen crush under their feet
a hyacinth in the mountains; on the ground
purple blooms . . .

50

(a)   to goldenhaired Phoibos whom Leto bore . . .
having mingled . . . with the mighty-named son of Kronos.
Artemis swore the god's great oath
      . . . (on her father's) head: "I will always be a virgin
5 . . . on mountain peaks
    . . . nod in assent for my sake."
      . . . the father of the blessed gods assented.
       . . . the gods . . . the Deer-Shooting Huntress
       . . . a great title.
10   . . . love never draws near.

(b)   shining . . . of the Muses . . .
makes . . . and of the Graces . . .
slender . . .
not to forget anger
5 for mortals . . .

51

the herald came . . .
Idaios . . . swift messenger
*
" . . . and the rest of Asia . . . unceasing fame:
5 Hektor and his friends bring a sparkling-eyed girl
from holy Thebes and everflowing Plakia—
delicate Andromache—in ships on the brine
sea; many gold bracelets, fragrant
purple robes, iridescent trinkets,
10 countless silver cups, and ivory."
So he spoke. Hektor's dear father leapt up;
the report reached friends through the wide city.
At once Trojan men harnessed mules
to the smooth-running carriages, a whole throng
15 of women and slender-ankled maidens stepped in;
apart from them, Priam's daughters . . .
and the unwed men yoked horses
to the chariots . . . , far and wide . . .
            . . . charioteers . . .

* * *

            . . . like gods
          . . . sacred gathering
hastened . . . to Troy,
the sweet melody of reed-pipe and [kithara] mingled,
25 sound of castanets, the maidens
sang a holy song, a silvery divine echo
reached the sky, [laughter] . . .
and everywhere through the streets . . .
mixing-bowls and drinking-bowls . . .
30 myrrh, cassia, and frankincense together.

The elder women all cried out "Eleleu,"
and all the men shouted high and clear
invoking Paion, the archer skilled in lyre,
and they praised Hektor and Andromache, godlike.   §§

52

There a bowl of ambrosia
had been mixed and Hermes,
taking a wine flask, poured for the gods.
They all held drinking-cups
5 and made libations; they prayed
all together for the bridegroom's prosperity.

53

. . . since yes you [were] once a child
. . . come on, sing these . . .
. . . talk, and favor us . . .
. . . abundantly,

5 for we are going to a wedding. And you . . .
this well, but as quick as possible . . .
send away virgins, and may the gods
keep . . .

. . . the road to great Olympos
10 . . . for humans . . .

54

§§ Happy bridegroom, the marriage that you prayed for
has been fulfilled—you have the girl you prayed for.
Your form is graceful, eyes . . .
gentle, and love flows over your alluring face
5 . . . Aphrodite has honored you above all.

55

There is no other girl, bridegroom, like this.

56

§§ With what, dear bridegroom, can I fairly compare you?
With a slender sapling I shall best compare you.

57

§§ Raise high the roof
—Hymen!—
you carpenter men.
—Hymen!—
5 The bridegroom approaches like Ares
—Hymen!—
much bigger than a big man.
—Hymen!

58

§§ The doorkeeper has feet seven fathoms long,
and sandals of five ox-hides—
the labor of ten cobblers.

59

Bride: Virginity, virginity, where have you gone leaving me behind?
Virginity: Never again will I come to you, never again.

60

Do I still desire virginity?

61

Night . . .

Virgins . . .
celebrate all night . . .
may sing of your love and
5   the violet-robed bride.
But once roused, go [call]
the unwed men your age
so we may see [less] sleep
than the clear-voiced [bird].   §§

62

§§ The full moon was rising,
and as women stood round the alter . . .

63

§§ Delicate Adonis is dying, Kytheria—what should we do?
Beat your breasts, daughters, and rend your dresses.

64

In the house of those who serve the Muses, a dirge
is not right . . . for us that wouldn't be proper.

65

I don't know what I should do—I'm of two minds.

66

I will now sing this beautifully
to delight my companions.

67

Come, divine lyre, speak to me,
take voice!

68

I say someone in another time will remember us.

ALKAIOS

1

I don't understand the conflict of the winds,
one wave rolls round from this side,
another from that, and we in the middle
with our black ship are carried along

5   struggling with the tremendous storm:
bilge rises above the masthold,
already the sail lets light through
and great rents run down it,

halyards give way and the rudders
10   ∗
    ∗
both feet stay . . .

in the sheets—this alone
saves me. The cargo . . .
15   . . . above . . .
   ∗

2

§§ . . . wretched me,
    I live a rustic life,
    longing to hear the assembly
    summoned, son of Agesilaos,

5   and the council. From what my father and my father's
    father have grown old possessing—among these
    citizens destroying each other—
    I have been driven away,

    an exile in the outskirts; like Onomakles,
10 here I settled alone in the wolf-thickets
    . . . war—because to give up the conflict
    against . . . is not better.

       . . . to the precinct of the blessed gods
       . . . walking on the black earth
15   . . . in the gatherings among women,
    I dwell, keeping my feet out of trouble,

    where the Lesbian women being judged for beauty
    promenade in trailing robes,
    and a divine echo rings out from the holy
20 cry of women each year.

    From many . . . when will the Olympian gods
    *
    *
    *   §§

3

[having done] most shameful, unjust things,
      . . . necessary to overthrow
      . . . by stoning.

      . . . far better for the Achaians
5 if they had killed . . .
then sailing past Aigai,
they'd have found the sea . . .

But in the temple Priam's daughter
      . . . clasped the chin
10   . . . of Athena, rich in warspoils,
while enemies invaded the city

      . . . and Daiphobos too
      . . . from the wall wailing
      . . . and the cry of children
15 filled the plain . . .

[But Ajax] came in a deadly, rabid madness
[to the temple of chaste] Pallas, who is
[most terrible] to god-robbing mortals
of all the blessed gods.

20 Seizing the virgin with both [hands]
as she stood by the . . . statue,
the Lokrian [raped] her; he did not fear
[the daughter of Zeus], giver of war,

. . . But with a terrible frown
    . . . livid, she darted over the wine-dark
sea and suddenly stirred up
unseen hurricanes.

4

§§   Come to me, leaving the Peloponnesos
    . . . sons of Zeus and Leda
with . . . spirit appear, Kastor
and Polydeukes,

5   who come over the wide earth
and entire sea on swift horses
and easily rescue men from chilling
death,

darting to the tops of well-fitted ships
10   from far away, radiant . . .
and in the difficult night bringing light
to the black ship . . .

5

The story goes, from evil . . .
for Priam and his sons . . .
from you bitter . . .
holy Troy.

5   Not such a woman the son of Aiakos . . .
calling all the Blessed Ones to his wedding,
led out of Nereus' house, taking
the gentle virgin

to the house of Cheiron, and he loosened
10 the virgin's belt. Love . . .
of Peleus and the best of Nereus' daughters.
Within a year

she bore a child, of demigods . . .
fortunate driver of tawny mares,
15 but those were destroyed and their city
for the sake of Helen.   §§

6

. . . and excited the heart of Argive
Helen; maddened by the Trojan man,
a traitorous guest, she followed him
in a ship on the sea,

5   leaving at home her child . . .
and her husband's richly covered bed . . .
her heart persuaded by love . . .
daughter of Zeus and Leda

   *

10 . . . many of his brothers . . .
. . . the Trojan plain holds conquered
because of that woman,

many chariots in the dust . . .
. . . and many lively-eyed men . . .
15   . . . slaughter . . .
   *

7

§§ Drink . . . with me, Melanippos. Why (think that)
once across great eddying Acheron . . .

you will see the sun's pure light again?
Come, don't [aim at] great things.

5 Even Sisyphos, son of Aiolos, king . . .
most cunning of men . . .

but even with his wisdom, by fate twice
he crossed over eddying Acheron . . .

the son of Kronos, King Zeus, gave him a task
10 under the black earth. Come, don't . . .

now if ever, while we are young . . .
. . . to experience whatever of these . . .

8

§§ Wet your lungs with wine—the dogstar rises,
and the season is harsh,
everything thirsts in the heat,
from the leaves a cicada chirps sweetly . . .
5 the artichoke flowers; now women are most pestilent
and men weak, since Sirius parches head
and knees . . .

IBYKOS

1

In Spring, quince trees
irrigated with streams
from rivers, in the Virgins'
inviolate garden, and vinebuds
5 growing beneath shady shoots
of vinetwigs bloom. But for me
Love rests for no season:
blazing with lightning
Thracian Boreas,
10 darting from Kypris, dark
with parching madness, shameless,
violently shakes
my senses from the depth.

2

Again Love, glancing meltingly
beneath royal blue eyelids,
with myriad enchantments throws me
into the infinite nets of Kypris.
5   Yes, I tremble at his approach,
as a yoke-bearing horse,
   a prizewinner near old age,
goes to the contest unwillingly
   with the swift chariots.

3

On its highest leaves
sit iridescent ducks with shiny necks,
and purple birds
and halcyons with slender wings.

4

" . . . and I killed the Molione boys,
twins on white horses,
same age two heads one body
both born in a silver
egg."

5

. . . they destroyed the famous and wealthy
and great city of Dardanus' son Priam,
dashing out from Argos,
by great Zeus' design

5   having a richly sung conflict
about blond Helen's form
in a tear-stained war,
and ruin mounted much-suffering Pergamon
because of goldenhaired Kypris.

10 Now I desire to sing
neither of Paris, traitorous guest,
nor of slender-ankled Kassandra
and the other children of Priam,

and high-gated Troy's unspeakable
15 day of capture; nor . . .
the surpassing excellence
of heroes whom the well-riveted

hollow ships brought
as an evil for Troy, the noble heroes;
20 the ruler Agamemnon led them,
descendant of Pleisthenes, king, leader of men,
son sprung from noble Atreus.

The skilled Muses of Helikon
could well embark on such a story,

25 but no living, mortal man
    could tell all the details,

    how great a number of ships from Aulis
    through the Aegean sea from Argos
    came to horse-rearing
30 Troy, and in them men

    with bronze shields, sons of Achaians,
    of whom the most excellent with the spear
                    . . . swift-footed Achilles
    and the great son of Telamon, valiant Ajax
35 *

            . . . most beautiful from Argos
                . . . Kyanippos to Ilion
    *

    *

40   . . . gold-girt
    Hyllis bore, to whom Trojans
    and Danaans found Troilos
    very similar in lovely form,

    just as gold, already
45 thrice-refined, to orichalcum—
    these partake in everlasting beauty.
    And you, Polykrates, will have undying fame
    through song and my fame.   §§

ANAKREON

1

(a)   Come, boy, bring us
     a bowl, so I can drink
     a long draught, pouring in ten
     ladles of water, and five
5 of wine, so that I may again
     tastefully break out in Bacchic frenzy.

(b)   Come again, let us no longer,
     with clatter and shouting
     over the wine, practice
     Scythian drinking, but drink
5 moderately amid lovely songs.

2

I implore you, deer-shooter,
light-haired daughter of Zeus,
queen of wild beasts, Artemis;
who now, somewhere by the eddies
5   of Lethaios, look down on
the city of bold-hearted men
and rejoice, since you shepherd
such a temperate people.

3

O Lord, with whom subduer Love
and dark-eyed Nymphs
and rosy Aphrodite
play, and you wander
5   the high peaks of mountains:
I implore you—come to us
kindly—to hear my prayer
and find it pleasing:
be a good counsellor
10   to Kleoboulos, Dionysos,
bid him accept my love.

4

Tossing a crimson ball
again, goldenhaired Love
challenges me to play
with the girl in fancy sandals.
5   But she, since she's from well-founded
Lesbos, finds fault with
my hair, since it's white
and she gapes after another girl.

5

Lad, glancing like a virgin,
I seek you, but you don't hear,
not knowing that you
are my soul's charioteer.

6

Soaring again from the Leukadian Rock
I dive into the grey waves, drunk with love.

7

The dice of Love are
madness and turmoil.

8

Again Love struck me like a smith with a giant
hammer, and washed me in a wintry torrent.

9

Thracian filly, why do you
look with eyes askance
and stubbornly flee me, and why
do you think I've no skill?
5 Understand this: I could well
throw a bridle on you,
and holding the reins I could turn
you round the goal of the track.
But now you graze the meadows
10 and, frisking nimbly, play,
since you've no dextrous horseman,
no easy rider.

10

Already my temples are grey
and head white,
graceful youth is no longer
here, but teeth are old,
5   no longer is much time left
of sweet life.

Because of these things, I weep,
often afraid of Tartaros;
for the recess of Hades is terrible,
10 and the descent to it
difficult, and it is certain that
he who has gone down can't come up.

11

not . . .
but near another you have a timid
heart, lovely-faced child;

and she thinks . . .
5   holding you close . . .
to rear, . . .

the hyacinth fields,
where Kypris bound her mares
       . . . by their yoke straps;

10   . . . in the middle, you shattered
       . . . so that many
of the citizens grew excited in their hearts.

You're a tramp, Herotima, a tramp . . .

SIMONIDES

1

Human strength
is puny, sorrows impossible,
in a short life labor upon labor—
and over all hangs inescapable Death:
5   good men and bad share
an equal portion of that.

2

Being human, don't ever say what happens tomorrow,
or seeing a man happy, how long he will be—
so swift not even the changing course
of a dragonfly.

3

All things come to one hideous Charybdis,
heroic excellence and wealth alike.

4

Thermopylai's dead
had glorious fortune—a noble fate,
their tomb an altar, for tears remembrance, for pity praise:
a shroud such as this, decay
5   nor all-conquering time will dim.
This sepulcher of good men took for attendant the acclaim
of Greece—and Leonidas too bears witness,
Sparta's king who left behind great adornment
of heroic excellence and everlasting fame.

5

Who, trusting his mind, could praise the man of Lindos, Kleoboulos,
who against everflowing rivers, spring flowers,
flame of sun and golden moon,
and churning sea, set the strength of a stele?
5   All things are weaker than gods—and stone
even mortal hands shatter. From a fool
came that counsel.

6

. . . distinguishes the fair and the shameful;
but if someone [slanders], having a mouth
without a door, his smoke is ineffectual—
gold is not stained,
5   truth all-powerful.
But to a few [the god] grants excellence
[effective] to the end: it's not easy to be good—
either irresistible gain
or the mighty gadfly of wile-weaving Aphrodite
10 and [thriving] desires for victory
force him against his will.
If throughout his life
            . . . he cannot hold to the lawful path,
        . . . as far as possible . . .
15   . . . crooked . . .
        . . . a just man . . .

7

It is hard to become a truly good
man, in hands, feet, and mind
made foursquare without flaw—
* * *

11 Pittakos' proverbial saying does not ring true
to me, although said by a wise man;
he said that it is hard to be good.
Only a god may keep that prize; it is not possible
15 for a man not to be bad
whom irresistible misfortune brings down:
if he fares well every man is good,
but bad if badly . . .
(For the most part, the best men are those
20 whom the gods love.)

So I will never throw out my portion of life
on an empty, impossible hope,
seeking what cannot be:
a wholly blameless human among us
25 who take fruit from the broadbased earth—
if I find him I'll tell you.
I praise and love all
who willingly do nothing
shameful—but with necessity
30 not even the gods fight.

*

*

(I'm not fond of blame, since for me he suffices
who isn't usually bad) or too inept,

35 knowing justice that helps the state,
a sound, healthy man—him I will not
blame, for countless
is the race of fools.
All things are fair in which
40 shameful things are not mixed. §§

8

Without pleasure,
what mortal life is desirable?
what tyrant's power?
Without her, not even the gods' lifespan is enviable.

9

As whenever
in a wintry month, Zeus
makes fourteen days behave,
men on earth call it
5 the season escaping wind,
sacred and nurturing the young
of the many-hued halcyon.

10

When in the skillfully welded chest,
wind blowing and rocking sea
threw her down
in fear, cheeks wet with tears,
5   around Perseus she put a loving hand
and said: "Child, I have such trouble—
but you sleep well, in your suckling
way you slumber deeply
in this joyless bronzebolted boat
10 gleaming in the night,
stretched out in the murky blue darkness—
you don't care about the high
froth of the waves
washing above your hair nor the voice
15 of the wind, lying in your purple
cloak, fair face [showing].
If to you the terrible were terrible,
you would hold my words
in your little ear.
20 But I urge you sleep my baby,
and let the sea sleep, sleep our boundless evil:
may some change of heart appear,
Father Zeus, from you—
and if my prayer is too bold
25 or without justice,
forgive me."

11

They wept for the violet-wreathed [lady's]
suckling baby breathing out its sweet life.

12

No leaf-shaking blast of winds
then arose, that spreading about
would have kept his honeysweet voice
from fastening in the ears of mortals.

13

Countless birds
swooped over Orpheus' head,
and fish leapt straight up
from the deepblue water
5   at his beautiful song.

14

There is a tale
that Excellence lives on inaccessible rocks,
keeping to her holy place—
nor is she visible to the eyes of all
5   mortals, for whom heart-biting sweat
does not come from within
and who do not reach that peak of prowess.

KORINNA

1

Terpsichore [told] me
lovely old tales to sing
to the white-robed women of Tanagra
and the city delighted greatly
5   in my voice, clear as the swallow's.

Since whatever great . . .
false . . .
. . . land with wide dancing-places,
and stories from our fathers' time
10   by my art adorned
for the young women [I'll begin].

Many times I adorned
the leader Kephisos with stories—
often, too, the great Orion
15   and his fifty strong sons
from his mingling with nymphs
. . . Libya . . .

*
I tell of the girl . . .

20 lovely to see . . .
the [land] bears . . .
. . . I bore . . .

2

"The Kouretes hid the goddess's
heavenly infant in a cave
secret from the crooked mind of Kronos
when blessed Rhea stole him,

5 and from the Immortals she gained
great honor." There he ended his song.
At once the Muses ordered
the blessed gods to bring their secret
ballot stones to the gold-glistening
10 urns, and they all arose together.

Kithairon gained the larger share.
Swiftly Hermes with a shout
announced that he had gained
the desired victory; with wreaths
15 the blessed gods . . .
adorned him, and his mind delighted.

But Helikon, gripped by
harsh griefs,
[ripped out] a bare boulder,
20 and the mountain . . . Groaning pitiably
. . . from on high he dashed it
down into countless shattered stones.

3

"Of your daughters: Zeus, Father
and King of all, has three;
three, the Lord of the Sea,
Poseidon, wed; Phoibos
5 rules over the beds of two;

and Maia's skillful son,
Hermes, one. Eros and Kypris
persuaded them, so they went
secretly into your house,
10 to steal the nine girls.

Your girls will yet bring forth
a race of heroes, demigods—
they will be both fruitful
and unaging; (this I know)
15 from the oracular tripod.

[I received] this gift, I
out of fifty strong brothers,
supreme prophet, Akraiphen,
whose allotment, from the revered
20 inner sanctuary, is truth.

The son of Leto first let
Euonomos prophesy
from the oracular seat.
Hyrieus, expelling him from
25 his land, next held this honor—

he was Poseidon's son.
Then did Orion, my father,
after regaining his land:
now he lives in heaven
30 and the honor [is mine].

       . . . therefore I tell
the true prophetic tale.
But now yield to the Immortals
and set free . . . your mind,
35 as Father-in-law of gods."

So spoke the respected prophet.
Asopos, having gladly taken
him by the right hand,
letting fall a tear from his eyes,
40 replied with these words: . . .

4

Are you sleeping endlessly? You never did before, Korinna.

5

And you, happy man, grandson of Kronos,
Poseidon's son, you, lord Boiotos . . .

6

Wishing to take her son
in her loving embrace . . .

7

Mighty Orion conquered
and called all the land
by his own name.

8

That grudging man [can't hurt] you . . .

9

I blame even clear-voiced
Myrtis; I do because, though born
a woman, she competed with Pindar.

10

But I sing the excellence of heroes
male and female . . .

11

Over you, Hermes fights
against Ares . . .

12

Daughter of Hyria, land of lovely dances . . .

13

Thespia, bearing a beautiful race, stranger-loving, Muse-beloved . . .

14

But let one of you hear this . . .

15

. . . leaving the [streams] of Ocean
. . . the holy light of the moon
. . . and the season from immortal Zeus
. . . delight in flowers of spring.
. . . dance through seven-gated [Thebes] . . .

TELESILLA

1

But Artemis, my girls,
fleeing Alpheos . . .

PRAXILLA

1

The fairest thing I leave behind is sunlight,
then shining stars and the full moon's face,
and also ripe cucumbers, and apples and pears.

2

Yet they never persuaded your heart.

3

Learning from the tale of Admetos, my friend, love the brave
but avoid cowards, knowing the gratitude of cowards is small.

4

Watch for a scorpion, my friend, under every stone.

5

You who look lovely from the windows—
a virgin face, but newly wed below . . .

ERINNA

1

              . . . girls,
              . . . brides,
              . . . tortoise
              . . . moon,
5   . . . tortoise,

   *

   *

              . . . in leaves

   *

10 *

          . . . I combed
       . . . into the [wide] wave
with mad feet [. . . leaped] from white horses.
"Aiai, I'm caught!" I cried out; [becoming] the tortoise
15 [I chased you round] the yard of the great court.
[Grieving] for you, poor Baukis, I lament these things,
these traces . . . lie warm in my heart
still; those . . . we played are coals now.
. . . and of dolls . . . in the bedrooms
20 brides . . . And near dawn
Mother . . . for the weavers;

she went to you . . . with salted . . .
For little ones . . . the Bogy brought fear—
. . . Mormo wandered about on four feet,
25 shape-shifting from one thing to [another].

But when into the bed . . . you forgot everything
that as a baby . . . you heard from your mother,
dear Baukis; Aphrodite . . . forgetfulness.
Because of this, weeping aloud for you, I leave [other things]:
30 my feet are not permitted . . . away from the house,
with my eyes [I may] not see you dead nor lament
with my hair unbound and wild . . . Blushing shame
rakes my [cheeks] . . .
but always before . . .
35 nineteenth [year] . . .
Erinna, dear . . .
gazing on the distaff . . .
Know that . . .
the spinning . . .
40 These things shame . . . me . . .
with virginal . . .
But looking . . .
and . . . soft-spoken
grey-haired women, those flowers of old age for mortals.
45 Because of this, dear . . .
Baukis, I weep aloud for you . . .
the flame . . .
hearing the keening . . .
O Hymen . . . often . . .
50 and often touching . . .
all for one, O Hymen . . .
Aiai, poor Baukis . . .

2

From here an empty echo penetrates to Hades;
but silence among the dead, and darkness closes their eyes.

3

Escort fish, Pompilos, sending sailors a fair sailing,
may you escort from the stern my sweet friend.

4

Stele and my sirens and mournful urn,
which holds the meager ashes belonging to Hades,
tell those passing by my tomb "farewell"
(be they townsmen or from other places)
5   and that this grave holds me, a bride. Say too,
that my father called me Baukis and my family
is from Tenos, so they may know, and that my friend
Erinna on the tombstone engraved this epigram.

5

I'm the tomb of Baukis, a bride; passing the deeply lamented
stele you may say this to underground Hades:
"You're malicious, Hades." To you who look, the fine letters
will announce the cruel fortune of Baukis:
5   how her father-in-law cremated the girl with fire
from the pine torches over which Hymen rejoiced.
And you, O Hymen, transformed the melody
of weddings to the sound of wailing dirges.

6

Delicate hands fashioned this portrait: good Prometheus,
there are even humans equal to you in skill.
If whoever painted this girl so true to life
had added a voice too, Agatharchis would be complete.

ANYTE

1

Stand there, manslaying spear; no longer drip
baneful enemies' gore around your bronze talon,
but resting against Athena's high marble temple
proclaim the prowess of Kretan Echekratidas.

2

An ox-sized cauldron, Kleubotos gave
(Eriaspis' son from wide-open Tegea);
the gift for Athena, Aristoteles made
(from Kleitor, allotted his father's name).

3

Lone Theudotos placed this gift beneath the mountain
peak for hair-raising Pan and the grotto Nymphs
because his great weariness from the holy harvest
they ended, holding out in their hands honeysweet water.

4

—Why, rustic Pan, sitting in the lone shady wood,
do you play this sweet-echoing reed pipe?
—So that along these dew-covered hills my calves
may pasture, culling from the fertile crops.

5

This is Kypris' place; it ever pleases her
to watch the sparkling sea from dry land,
so she may provide sailors a pleasant voyage—
the sea fears the sight of her gleaming statue.

6

I, Hermes, stand here by the windy tree-lined
crossroads near the white coastal water,
sheltering men weary from the road—
my fountain murmurs cold and clear.

7

Sit, everyone, under the luxuriant laurel;
draw sweet drink from the seasonal spring,
so your body, panting from harvest labors,
may rest, struck by the breath of Zephyros.

8

Stranger, below the boulder rest your spent limbs;
sweetly a breeze whispers to you in the fresh, green leaves.
Sip cold springwater from the stream: for travellers
in the burning heat this is a pleasant respite.

9

Putting red reins on you, goat, with a noseband
round your shaggy mouth, the children train you
in horse contests around the god's temple,
so long as you bear them gently to their delight.

10

Behold the horned goat of Bacchos, how lordly
he fixes a haughty eye down his shaggy jaw,
exulting how a Naiad in the mountains
often took his curly beard in her rosy hand.

11

No longer will I fling up my neck, exulting
in the buoyant seas arising from the deep,
nor around the ship's bow (with fine oarlocks)
do I blow, delighting in my figurehead:
5 the darkened seawater thrust me on land;
I lie beached by this shallow, sandy coast.

12

You, too, perished by a bush with tangled roots,
Lokrian hound, swiftest of noise-loving pups:
into your nimble leg a snake with gleaming
neck injected such pitiless poison.

13

No longer, as before, plying with whirring wings,
will you awaken me from bed at daybreak—
for as you slept, a marauder approaching secretly
killed you, one claw easily piercing your throat.

14

For the cricket (nightingale of the field) and oak-
dwelling cicada, Myro made a common grave,
the girl weeping a virgin tear, because immovable
Hades went away holding her two pets.

15

Damis erected this mound for his dead steadfast
horse, after Ares struck its bloodied bay chest—
its dark blood burst through the tough hide
and drenched the ploughed soil with gore.

16

The youth buried you, Captain; as sons for their mother,
Pheidias, when you died you cast them into gloomy grief,
while the stone above you sings this fine epitaph—
how you died fighting for your dear fatherland.

17

This Lydian earth covers Amyntor, Philip's son,
who often engaged his hands in iron battle:
no painful disease led him to the House of Night,
but he perished covering a comrade with his round shield.

18

Often keening on her daughter's tomb, Kleina
cried aloud for her swiftly-doomed dear child,
evoking the soul of Philainis, who unwed
passed over Acheron's fresh, pale stream.

19

I mourn maiden Antibia: desiring her, many
bridegrooms came to her father's home, drawn
by her fame for beauty and wit. But in the end
destructive Fate rolled far away the hopes of all.

20

Throwing her arms around her dear father,
fresh tears flowing, Erato spoke these final words:
"Father, I'm yours no more, but already dead;
murky black Thanatos clouds my sight."

21

Instead of bridal bed and holy wedding songs
for you, on this marble tomb your mother
set a virgin your image in size and beauty,
Thersis; so you are greeted even though dead.

22

We go, Miletos, dear fatherland, spurning
the lawless violence of godless Gauls;
three virgins, your citizens, whom the forceful
Celtic Ares turned to this fate:
5   we did not wait for unholy blood, or bridal
song, but found Hades our guardian.

23

This Manes alive once was a slave; now dead,
his power equals that of great Darius.

NOSSIS

1

Nothing is sweeter than love, all other riches
second: even honey I've spat from my mouth.
This Nossis says: Whomever Kypris hasn't kissed
knows nothing of her flowers, what sort of roses.

2

Stranger, if you sail to the land of lovely dances, Mitylene,
to catch fire from the blossom of Sappho's graces,
say that a friend to her and the Muses, the Lokrian land
bore me. And knowing my name is Nossis, go on!

3

Shields Bruttians threw from their doomed shoulders—
struck by the hands of Lokrians quick in battle—
lie in the gods' shrines, praising their bravery,
not longing for the cowards' forearms they left.

4

O Honored Hera, who often descending from heaven
view your incense-scented Lakinian shrine,
take the linen robe that Kleocha's daughter Theuphilis
wove for you with her noble child Nossis.

5

When we go to the temple, let's see Aphrodite's
statue, skillfully worked with gold.
Polyarchis erected it, having reaped so much
gain from her body's own splendor.

6

It seems that Aphrodite took with joy
this hairband, an offering from Samytha—
it's skillfully worked and smells sweetly of nectar,
with which the goddess too anoints fair Adonis.

7

Kallo dedicated her portrait in the house of golden
Aphrodite, the picture painted true to life.
How gentle her stance, see how her grace blossoms!
Greet her with joy, for she has a blameless life.

8

This portrait captures Thaumareta's form—it renders
well the spirit and youth of the gentle-eyed woman.
The house watchpup, looking at you, might wag her tail,
thinking she sees the mistress of the house.

9

Melinna herself is re-created: notice the face
is gentle; she seems to gaze serenely at us.
How truly the daughter resembles her mother in all—
how fine when children are like their parents.

10

Even from a distance, this picture is known
by its form and majesty to be of Sabaithis.
Look closer—I think I can see her wit
and serenity. May you fare well, blessed woman.

11

When you've laughed out loud and said a friendly
word to me, pass by. I am Rhinthon of Syracuse,
a little nightingale of the Muses, but from
tragic burlesques I picked my own ivy crown.

12

O Artemis of Delos and lovely Ortygia,
lay down your pure archery in the laps of the Graces;
washing your skin clean in Inopos, enter the house
to deliver Alketis from difficult labor.

MOIRO

1

Great Zeus was reared in Krete and no one
of the Blessed knew him; he grew in all his limbs.
The timid birds nursed him in a holy cave
bringing ambrosia from the streams of Ocean;
5   and a great eagle, ever drawing nectar from a rock,
would bring drink in his beak for cunning Zeus.
So after thundering Zeus conquered his father Kronos,
he had the eagle dwell in heaven, immortal;
so too he provided honor for the timid doves,
10 who are truly the heralds of summer and winter.

2

Beneath Aphrodite's golden portico you now lie,
Grape-cluster, swollen with a drop of Dionysos;
your mother, throwing round her loving branch,
will no longer grow a fragrant leaf above your head.

3

Tree nymphs, daughters of River, ambrosial
beings who on rosy feet ever walk these depths,
fare well and protect Kleonymos, who erected these fine
wooden statues for you, goddesses, beneath the pines.

HEDYLA

1

Either cockleshells from the Erythraian reef as gifts
or still unfledged halcyon chicks
as delights for the nymph [Glaukos gave], without hope.
Even the Siren, a neighboring maiden,
5 pitied his tears; for she swam to that shore
and close to those of Aetna.

MELINNO

1

Hail, Roma, daughter of Ares,
gold-banded warrior queen,
who dwells on earth in sacred Olympos
ever indestructible.

5   To you alone, Eldest, has Fate
given royal glory of unbreakable rule,
that with sovereign strength
you might lead the way.

Under your yoke of strong straps,
10 breasts of earth and white-capped sea
are bound together: without stumbling
you steer the cities of peoples.

The greatest span of time—making all things fall
and molding life now in one way, now in another—
15 for you alone does not change the wind
filling the sails of rule.

Indeed, out of all, you alone bear
the strongest men, great spearwielders,
making a crop of men spring up
20 like the rich corn crops of Demeter.

Abbreviations

Bremer   Bremer, J. M., A. M. van Erp Taalman Kip, and S. R. Slings. *Some Recently Found Greek Poems*. Leiden and New York, 1987.

EG   Page, D. L. *Epigrammata Graeca*. Oxford, 1975.

Geoghegan   Geoghegan, D. *Anyte: The Epigrams*. Rome, 1979.

Giangrande   Giangrande, G. "An Epigram of Erinna." *CR* n.s. 19 (1969): 1–3.

Gow-Page   Gow, A. S. F., and D. L. Page. *The Greek Anthology: Hellenistic Epigrams*. Vols. 1 and 2. Cambridge, 1965.

PMG   Page, D. L. *Poetae Melici Graeci*. Oxford, 1962.

Powell   Powell, J. U. *Collectanea Alexandrina*. Oxford, 1925.

SLG   Page, D. L. *Supplementum Lyricis Graecis*. Oxford, 1974.

Supp. Hell.   Lloyd-Jones, H., and P. Parsons. *Supplementum Hellenisticum*. Berlin, 1983.

Voigt   Voigt, E. M. *Sappho et Alcaeus: Fragmenta*. Amsterdam, 1971.

West   West, M. L. *Delectus ex Iambis et Elegis Graecis*. Oxford, 1980.

Notes

ARCHILOCHOS

Archilochos (c. 680–640) is the author of the earliest surviving poetry in the "lyric" first person. Born on the island of Paros, Archilochos moved north to Thasos and fought in battles there against the Thracians. His father, Telesikles, had helped colonize Thasos a generation earlier. Archilochos at some point returned to Paros, and was killed in battle defending Paros from the neighboring island Naxos. A sanctuary was dedicated to him on Paros.

Archilochos wrote poetry of many types in his Ionian vernacular, the common dialect of the southern half of the Aegean Sea and west coast of Asia Minor. His poems are heavily enriched with epic formulas, the building blocks of oral epic. These epic echoes lend the authority of antiquity, yet also create a contrast to the formulas' new contexts.

Archilochos was famous in antiquity for his innovative use of meter and his invective (blame) poetry. Some of the names in his poetry are those of contemporary people, such as Glaukos and Perikles. Other names, such as Lykambes and Neobule, are more likely to be legendary than historical. Archilochos' use of lampoons and invective was later interpreted as straight autobiography— including the story that his mother was a slave, and the story of his deadly affair with Neobule. According to pseudobiography based on Archilochos' poetry, Lykambes promised his daughter Neobule in marriage to Archilochos, but then changed his mind. Thereupon Archilochos wrote scurrilous poetry, which drove Lykambes and Neobule to suicide. This fiction may seem plausible in light of the Greek emphasis on competition, reputation, and honor (see Winkler 1990). However, invective poetry was not actually expected to kill its victims (see Nagy 1979).

All of the Greek texts translated here survive in quotations, except for 20, which was recently discovered on papyrus and first published in 1974.

Archilochos 1: West 1
1. War Lord: Ares is the god of war.
2. The Muses' gift is poetry.

Archilochos 2: West 114

Archilochos 3: West 5
The speaker rejects the heroic ethic of not returning from battle without one's armor. The negatives, in lines 2 and 4, emphasize that he would rather not have left the shield—it is a shame to lose a perfectly good shield—but what was bought once can be bought again. A shield is replaceable; a man is not.
1. Thracian: The Greek is "Saians," a Thracian tribe. Thracians were considered wild and barbaric.

Archilochos 4: West 128
There are some uncertainties in the text (lines 2 and 3). A man should aim for moderation in his emotions because human fortune continually shifts from good to bad and back again. See Archilochos 5 and 6.
4–5. victory, defeat: In Greek, they are the active and passive of the same word, "conquering" and "being conquered."

Archilochos 5: West 130
The opening phrase is uncertain, either as I have it or "the gods arrange/establish everything" or even "all things are easy for the gods." Men's fortunes fluctuate; the gods rescue men in trouble and unseat men who were well established.

Archilochos 6: West 13
There will be no private or public celebrations because of mourning for the drowned men. (See Adkins, 35–44, for a complete discussion.) The grieving is appropriate, but must then be put aside.
7. drug: The Greek word, *pharmakon*, means either poison or medicine. The *pharmakon* of endurance does not cure the pain, but makes it bearable.

Archilochos 7: West 122

According to Aristotle, the poetic persona here is a father speaking about his daughter; if so, that information must have been in the missing ending of the poem. The poem probably refers to the total eclipse of April 6, 648.

4. damp: While the manuscript has "baneful" (*lugron*), Campbell (1967) rejects it on metrical grounds; he accepts "watery/damp" (*hugron*). "Damp fear" is a striking image whether it refers to "fear that turns men's limbs to water" (Campbell 1967, 155), or fear that makes men sweat, or fear itself as a damp, clammy, fluid thing.

7–9. After seeing the eclipse, anything seems possible, even land animals taking to the sea and dolphins to the mountains.

Archilochos 8: West 105

The storm probably is a metaphor for civil strife (*stasis*) as in Alkaios 1.

Archilochos 9: West 115 Hipponax

West attributes this poem to Hipponax, other editors to Archilochos. The speaker curses a man who betrayed his friendship.

2. barbaric: The Greek here actually says "top-knotted," referring to a characteristic Thracian hairstyle with the hair knotted or piled on top of the head.

Archilochos 10: West 19

According to Aristotle, the person speaking was Charon the carpenter.

1. Gyges: Gyges was the king (*tyrannos*) of Lydia, c. 687 to c. 652. Lydia was a wealthy and exotic kingdom east of the Greek world.

Archilochos 11: West 174

Fragments 11–13 are from a fable about a fox and an eagle. In this story, as retold by Aesop, the eagle betrays the fox by eating its cubs; retribution follows when the eagle brings a burning piece of meat from an altar to his nest. The nest catches fire, and the young eagles fall and are eaten by the fox.

Archilochos 12: West 176

Perhaps a third animal speaks to the fox about the eagle.

Archilochos 13: West 177

The fox prays for revenge on the eagle.

Archilochos 14: West 201

The fox has many tricks, but the hedgehog knows just one very effective trick: when it curls into a ball, the sharp spines on its back bristle out into a hedgelike defense.

Archilochos 15: West 30 and 31

These two fragments are quoted in separate sources, but seem to fit together.

Archilochos 16: West 193

Archilochos 17: West 191

Archilochos 18: West 118

Archilochos 19: West 196

This might be from the missing beginning of Archilochos 20.

1. limb-loosening: In Greek poetry, limbs relax in sleep, death, and love (especially after sex). See Sappho 16.

2. desire conquers: The Greek poets depict desire or Eros as an outside force that conquers one. The verb "conquer/dominate" is also used of taming an animal, killing a man in battle, or mastering a woman. See Sappho 18.

Archilochos 20: SLG S 478

Refer to Bremer for the most up-to-date and useful Greek commentary. This is the longest extant fragment of Archilochos' poetry. The right side of the papyrus is torn, rendering some line endings illegible. Some line beginnings are also uncertain.

In this erotic epode, the narrator quotes a dialogue between himself and a young woman (the daughter of Amphimedo) and tells what happened afterward. The fragment begins with the woman urging restraint: if he cannot wait, he should direct his passion elsewhere. She mentions a possible substitute, Neobule, who is presumably (the end of the line is missing) interested in the narrator. The narrator replies that he will act with restraint if Amphimedo's daughter will let him approach her sexually in some manner (lines 10–24). He rejects the offer of Neobule, contrasting the two women and his actions in regard to them: Neobule is a whore and his past behavior, perhaps with Neobule, was as hasty and excessive as his present invective against her, while this young woman is a maiden and he will act with moderation. The narrator then describes how he instigated some kind of sexual contact with his desired woman.

Gentili (186–90) proposes that the scene takes place in a sanctuary of Hera, the goddess of marriage, and that the women mentioned are her priestesses. Therefore, the sexual contact described at the end of the poem is sacrilegious and would shame her family.

Felson-Rubin says that the poem allows for the "development of the male narrator from potentially unrestrained to restrained by (1) providing a legitimate . . . outlet for his emotional excess and by (2) allowing him to objectify and disown certain character traits ascribed to Neobule" (136–37).

1–8. The fragment begins mid-sentence into the woman's reply.

6. woman: *Parthenos* means a marriageable young woman, not necessarily physically a virgin in our sense. The Greek word is the same in lines 27 ("virgin") and 42 ("girl"), while in line 30 ("woman"), the word is *gynē*, a "mature woman."

8. West suggests "your own" for the missing words.

14. goddess: Aphrodite.

15. aside from the divine thing: This phrase means other than full sexual intercourse. (See Van Sickle, 137–43, for a fuller discussion.) The narrator says that a "delight" other than full intercourse will suffice for him.

21–23. cornice, gates, garden grass: These are among the many Greek sexual metaphors for the female genital area. (See Bremer, 39, for commentary on this passage.) More literally, they refer to the setting, perhaps a temple sanctuary.

25. Neobule: The use of her name here shows that the narrator knew who was meant, in line 4, by the "woman in our house."

29. She couldn't get her fill: The papyrus has only "for . . . no . . . satiety."

30. Only half of a word is legible; the best two possibilities are "youth" and "ruin." The parallel with lines 49–50 contrasts the spent youth of Neobule with the maiden's fresh bloom of youth.

32. Perhaps the partially visible word means "happen" or "be at hand"; see Bremer, 42–43.

38. West suggests "her own" for the missing words.

39–41. I fear . . . bitch's litter: A proverb. If he acted hastily, he would beget literal or figurative offspring that would "miss the right day," or be inappropriate. As Felson-Rubin says, " . . . he fears not the birth of bastard children, but the products of untimeliness and haste, namely, another relationship like the one with Neobule or a renewed relationship with Neobule" (139).

47. like a fawn: Fawns freeze when in danger or when their mother is absent (her mother, Amphimedo, is dead), depending on their protective coloring to hide them from predators.

52–53. Because of the woman's fear, Archilochos leads us to expect a rape scene, the traditional outcome in Greek literature of an erotic encounter in an erotic poem. The narrator does seem to keep his promise not to go all the way, that something aside from the "divine thing" would do (line 15). He seems to ejaculate while touching her pubic hair with his penis, or perhaps just by caressing her head hair with his hand. Thus, according to Felson-Rubin, the narrator does not, after all, give way to the excesses that he feared and that inspired his invective against Neobule. Yet although the narrator describes his touch as gentle, the woman's fear is evidence that whether or not penetration occurs, she is still portrayed as his conquest.

ALKMAN

When Alkman wrote his choral songs in the late seventh century, Sparta was a lively center for the arts. Religious festivals and contests of all sorts were celebrated with pageantry and splendor. Some of this richness is reflected in Alkman's partheneia, songs for choirs of young women of marriageable age. Sometimes the choirs sang in choral contests. In Sparta, women were active participants in a wide variety of competitive and noncompetitive public performances, including athletic and beauty contests. Two partheneia (1 and 2) have been discovered on papyrus; the other poems survive as quotations. All are in the local Lakonian dialect of Sparta.

Alkman 1: PMG 1

Partheneion 1 probably was performed in a state festival celebrating a particular goddess. The goddess mentioned in the poem is called Orthria and Aotis, names not otherwise known. The names evoke dawn or early morning. Orthria and Aotis might be cult names for a familiar goddess, such as Artemis, Aphrodite, or Helen (who was worshiped as a goddess in Sparta). Calame (1977) argues convincingly that Helen is the goddess meant. He speculates that this poem was sung as part of the ritual in a cult of Helen, in which the young women celebrate their passage from adolescence to adulthood. (See Calame 1977 and 1983 for a thorough study of Alkman and partheneia.)

This fragment opens with two myths (the second myth barely there at all), each followed by gnomic reflections. The first myth begins near the end of a tale recounting a battle between the Dioscuri and the ten sons of Hippocoon. The sons were killed in that battle. The first maxim (line 16) warns against going beyond one's destiny by trying to marry a goddess. The second myth, which could be a continuation of the first, provides little information. The maxim at line 36 concludes that the gods punish men for "evil deeds." The mythic past then gives way to the present in the second section of the poem. Here the poem praises ten young women, primarily Hagesichora, the chorus leader, and Agido, her companion.

Determining the occasion and meaning of the poem has stimulated a wide variety of responses. References to dawn and marriage may imply that it was originally performed at dawn and perhaps was an epithalamion (wedding song; see Griffith). The poem may have been performed in some kind of choral context, or been part of a noncompetitive performance. I see no textual evidence for rival choruses. Page, however, argues in favor of the Peleiades (line 60) as a rival chorus (1951, 57–62); Segal sums up the evidence against a rival chorus (261–62) and argues for rivalry between the leaders and the rest of the chorus (266); Davison sees rivalry between the two leaders (154).

1–12. The sons of Hippocoon, legendary Spartan heroes, were killed in a battle against the Dioscuri (Kastor and Polydeukes). Ten sons are listed as dead, five in the missing parts of lines 4–12. In one of the many conflicting versions of the myth, they fought because one of Hippocoon's sons seized Helen, the sister of the Dioscuri. This version best fits the context, since the maxim beginning at line 16 warns mortals against attempting to marry goddesses (including Aphrodite), and Helen was worshiped as a goddess at Sparta. (See Davison, 148–52, for versions and sources of the myth.)

2. Lykaithos: Although he died in the battle, he is not counted because he is not one of Hippocoon's sons, who were worshiped as heroes at Sparta. The Spartans remember and honor the sons of Hippocoon, even though they were justly killed.

13–21. This gnomic passage illuminates the preceding myth: men should not overstep their mortal bounds by seeking to marry a goddess.

13. Destiny: *Aisa* is the divine personification of destiny. She assigns necessity and limits on each person.

Resource: *Poros* gives people some way or means of freedom within these restrictions.

18–19. Porkos: Porkos is a sea-god like Nereus. The missing parts named at least one other goddess.

20. Graces: The Graces were connected with the Dioscuri in Spartan cult. Their glances, "love-eyes," inspire desire (see also line 75).

22–35. This is either a continuation of the myth or another one with a similar conclusion. Some young men did something rash and as a result were dispatched with arrow and stone to Hades.

36–39. A second maxim provides a transition from the mythical past to the present, and from suffering to celebration.

38. weaves: *Aisa* weaves human destiny, but humans also weave the pattern of their own lives to their ends.

39. I sing: Alkman uses first person singular and plural interchangeably throughout the rest of the poem to refer to the whole chorus singing. The chorus probably consists of ten young women, since ten are named within the poem.

40. Agido: The poem praises Agido, one of the chorus, second only to the chorus leader.

radiance: This is the first of many images of light, appropriate in an invocation to a dawn goddess.

43–44. praise or blame: They say that the chorus leader does not want them to mention Agido, but, of course, they already have praised her. See lines 64–77 for praise framed in denials of praise. (Also, see Nagy 1979, 222–42 for discussion of praise and blame in archaic poetry.)

44. chorus leader: Hagesichora, whose name means "chorus leader."

45. she herself: Hagesichora.

49. dreams beneath the rock: Nagy (1990, 223–34) argues that the rock is the Leukadian (White) Rock (see Anakreon 6), and represents the boundary between "the conscious and the unconscious." The dreams come from below the rock: Hagesichora is the ideal woman envisioned in one's dreams. Of course, it could just mean the dreams one has snoozing in the shade of a boulder. However, the Greek might mean "winged" not "rock": a horse "of winged dreams."

50. you: The second person pronoun is a direct address to the audience.

50–51. racer: Agido is likened to an Enetic racer, which perhaps is a small, fast horse. There is a long tradition of horse imagery for young women viewed erotically (see Anakreon 9).

hair: This word is usually used of a horse's mane, which is consistent with the repeated equine imagery.

52. cousin: The chorus are not all cousins by relation, but a group composed of Spartan citizens.

58. second after Agido: In regard to beauty, Hagesichora comes first, then Agido, then whoever is next best in the chorus or the chorus as a whole.

59. Kolaxaian, Ibenian: The Kolaxaian (Scythian) and Ibenian (Lydian) horses are both good eastern horses. The horses run together, *with* each other, perhaps like the "trace-horse" (line 92), not *against* each other. The chorus do not compete against themselves; they must "run" together for the success of the song. See the introductory note to this poem, above, for other interpretations.

60. Peleiades: Alkman brings together imagery of birds and light in calling Hagesichora and Agido "these Peleiades," which means both "doves" and the constellation Pleiades. Doves were held sacred to Aphrodite. In myth, the Pleiades once were sisters who were turned into the constellation when they fled attempted rape. The constellation shines brightly as a group, not as individual stars.

61. Sirius: Like Sirius, which is the brightest star in the sky, Hagesichora and Agido, the Peleiades, shine brightest in the chorus. Sirius' baneful and destructive associations, however, contrast with the timidness of doves, perhaps alluding to the destructive potential of eros as illustrated in the preceding myth of Hippocoon's sons.

62. robe: A scholium glosses *pharos* as a plough, although it generally refers to a sacred robe dedicated to a goddess. While some scholars accept "plough," Calame (1977) provides a convincing argument for "robe." Robes are common offerings to goddesses, while ploughs are not attested as offerings at all. Furthermore, the poem provides no internal connection with a plough.

Orthria: The goddess of dawn or early morning whom the poem celebrates. Since neither Orthria nor Aotis (line 88) is recorded elsewhere, scholars speculate that they are cult names for Artemis, Helen, or Aphrodite.

63. fight with us: The Peleiades fight along with the rest of the chorus, not

against them (as also in line 59). Further metaphors of cooperation support this reading: "trace-horse" (line 92)—horses yoked together following a leader—and "navigator" guiding a ship (lines 94–95).

64–77. This strophe lists the other eight chorus members. Alkman displays their beauty through the technique of discounting it in comparison to Hagesichora's beauty. Without Hagesichora, the chorus would not be successful—their individual talents alone would not be sufficient. The young women are praised in erotic language.

66. snake: The "snake" is probably a ritual object, perhaps a bracelet.

73. Ainesimbrota: She is not part of the chorus; according to West (1965) she dispenses love potions.

77. overwhelms: Literally "wears me out," which has sexual connotations; the chorus are "worn out" with longing for Hagesichora.

88. Aotis: Aotis means "dawn," and she is probably the same goddess referred to as Orthria (line 61).

89. toils: The song is the "toil"—the goddess grants them success (lines 83–84), and Hagesichora leads them to the successful completion of the song. The danger of defeat is that the song might "screech in vain" (line 86) by not having the right effect on the goddess and audience.

100. she sings: Hagesichora.

Alkman 2: PMG 3

At least fifty lines are missing from the center of this partheneion. The missing lines may have recounted a myth, as in Alkman 1. The hints of erotic language in 1 are explicit here. The poem ends at line 90.

1. Muses: The poem begins with an invocation to the Muses, according to Page's supplement.

5. singing: The chorus, not the Muses, sing.

8. contest: The "contest" refers to an assembly or choral competition.

10. feet: The chorus members dance while they sing.

71. Kinyras: He was king of Kypros (Cyprus), which was famous for its perfumes.

73–74. Astymeloisa: Her name means "city's care" or "darling of the city."

Alkman 3: PMG 26

1. maidens: They are either the Muses, or the chorus of young women for whom Alkman composed.

2. kingfisher: The kingfisher (*kērulos*) sometimes is identified as the male halcyon, a mythical sea bird. The image may be of the male in his old age being carried by the female halcyons.

Alkman 4: PMG 56

6. you: It is a woman enacting this ritual.

7. slayer of Argos: Hermes.

Alkman 5: PMG 58

Easterling speculates that "Alcman is here actually introducing Eros the youth playing games into the literary tradition. . . . the playful Eros gave the poets a chance to be rude about love without giving offence to a powerful Olympian goddess" (41).

1. wild: "Wanton, lustful."

4. galingale: "It is a handsome plant with slender, very smooth stems topped by clusters of light reddish-brown spikelets. . . . its strong supple stems could have made it a useful plant for binding into a garland . . ." (Easterling, 38).

Alkman 6: PMG 59

These two fragments may be part of a single poem.

2. Kyprian: Aphrodite.

Alkman 7: PMG 89

STESICHOROS

Stesichoros lived in Himera, Sicily in the late seventh century. Stesichoros used the conventional Doric dialect and triadic structure of choral lyric. The structure consists of a repeated pattern of two stanzas (strophe, antistrophe) in the same meter, followed by a third stanza (epode) in a different meter. Even though his poems have a structure common to choral lyric, they may be monodic. His long, narrative poetry reads like epic in lyric meters. He was famous for his unusual versions of myths. Poems 1–3 and 5 (parts i, x, xi) are from quotations; 4, the rest of 5, and 6 are from papyri—the last two recently discovered.

Stesichoros 1: PMG 187

This fragment probably refers to the marriage of Helen and Menelaos.

1. quinces: "Kydonian apples" are associated with nuptials.

Stesichoros 2: PMG 223

Sappho 4 and Alkaios 5 and 6 present other views of Helen.

4. daughters of Tyndareos: Klytemnestra's husbands were Tantalos (in some stories), Agamemnon, and Aigisthos; Helen's were Theseus (in some versions), Menelaos, and Paris.

Stesichoros 3: PMG 192

This is part of Stesichoros' palinode in which he recants the stories he told of Helen in another poem or poems. In his palinode, he says that Helen herself did not actually sail with Paris to Troy—a phantom was substituted for her.

Stesichoros 4: PMG 209

This fragment is from Stesichoros' *Homeward Returns* (*Nostoi*), which told the stories of the journeys home of various Greek heroes after the Trojan War. Sections (a) and (b) are from the same poem but not directly consecutive.

(a) Telemachos visits Helen and Menelaos for news about his father (see *Odyssey* 4).

1. In the Greek, Helen is described as a *nymphē*, a youthful married woman or a bride. Helen interprets the omen for Telemachos.

3. messenger: A bird is the messenger—the omen of line 1.

6. The omen probably indicates that Telemachos should return because Odysseus already has appeared at home.

8. counsels of Athena: Odysseus follows Athena's plan.

9. crow: The crow is female, perhaps a sign of Athena.

10. Helen will not delay Telemachos from returning home.

11. Penelope: When Penelope sees Telemachos, he will be the omen of his father's return.

(b) The second column of the papyrus describes the parting gift, which was from Troy, of Menelaos ("the son of Pleisthenes") to Telemachos.

Stesichoros 5: SLG S 7–19

These fragments are from one long narrative poem, in which Stesichoros tells how Herakles steals Geryon's cattle as his tenth labor, killing the herdsman Eurytion and then Geryon himself. Geryon has three bodies connected at the trunk (three heads, three sets of arms and legs, etc.). The story is unusual in that it portrays Geryon sympathetically by focusing on his heroic decision to fight Herakles to regain his cattle and by narrating his mother's desperate entreaties.

My interpretation, ordering of the fragments, and prose commentary in between the fragments depend heavily on Page (1973). S9 and S18 are too fragmentary to translate.

i. S 7

1. Erytheia: Geryon lives on the island of Erytheia, in the far west where the sun sets.

ii. S 8

Eurytion and his mother went from his birthplace, Tartessos, to the island of the Hesperides. When Eurytion grew up, he became the herdsman of Geryon's cattle on Erytheia.

iii. S 10

Menoites, another herdsman in the area, reports to Geryon that he witnessed Herakles kill Eurytion and steal the cattle. He entreats Geryon not to pursue Herakles.

2. Kallirhoa: Geryon's mother is mortal.

3. Chrysaor: Geryon's father, Poseidon's son, is immortal.

iv. S 11

2. Answering him: Geryon replies to Menoites that he will fight Herakles. As the son of an immortal father and a mortal mother, Geryon doesn't know whether he is immortal. If Geryon is immortal then Herakles cannot kill him, and if he is mortal then it would be better to die in combat than live with the disgrace.

14. horned: The stolen cattle.

25. May this: Geryon prays that "this," the theft of his cattle, does not have the gods' approval.

v. S 12

2. she saw: Geryon's mother, Kallirhoa, watches his arrival.

6. Obey: She entreats him to obey her wish that he not fight.

9. Aegis: The aegis, a sign of Zeus' and Athena's power, is a short cloak or shield.

vi. S 13

Kallirhoa continues her attempt to persuade him by reminding him that she is the mother who fed him. Her speech ends at line 8.

vii. S 14

Athena, who protects Herakles, asks Poseidon not to protect his grandson, Geryon.

8. The missing words probably were "not to save."

viii. S 15

From a safe distance Herakles knocks off Geryon's helmet and, in column (b) of the papyrus, shoots him in the head with a poison arrow.

(b)

3. its head: The arrowhead. Stesichoros focuses on the action of the arrow instead of on Herakles shooting the arrow.

4–6. The arrowhead is poisoned with blood and bile from the Hydra.

14–17. Stesichoros uses a strangely delicate simile in comparing Geryon's head stuck through with an arrow to a poppy (see *Iliad* 8.306–8).

ix. S 16

x. S 17

Herakles sailed to Erytheia in a great bowl lent him by the Sun and he sails back to Tartessos to return it after stealing the cattle.

1. son of Hyperion: The Sun.

8. son of Zeus: Herakles.

xi. S 19

This fragment may be from Herakles' journey home to Tiryns.

Stesichoros 6: Bremer (F)

The remaining fragment begins two hundred lines into the poem. Stesichoros tells how Jocasta attempts to settle peacefully the dispute between her sons, Eteokles and Polyneikes, over Oedipus' inheritance. She tries to forestall the destiny Teiresias foretells—that her sons will kill each other and bring ruin to Thebes. Jocasta is an intelligent queen who develops and suggests a logical way out: the brothers should divide kingship and possessions by lot. As a result, Eteokles wins the kingship and Polyneikes leaves Thebes with the goods.

Stesichoros' effective use of the repetitious language he was known for in antiquity can be discerned even in this fragmentary text. For instance, Jocasta manipulates language—"predict/prophesy" and "fulfill" (lines 2, 10, 13, 19)—in an attempt to manipulate her sons' destiny. Another repetition, however, implies that she will be unsuccessful: the word *neikos* (strife/quarrel) appears twice (lines 5, 33), reiterating the root of Polyneikes' name, "much strife."

1. Jocasta asks Teiresias not to tell her any prophecies—she does not need any new sorrows or fears to add to her current ones. The word for "fears" (line 3) is also "hopes."

9–10. She prays that Apollo not fulfill this one prophecy that Teiresias has given her.

15. The Greek in this line is suspect.

17. city: Thebes.

20. house: Jocasta's solution is that one son stay in the palace and, presumably, rule.

23–24. According to Parsons, "They are to shake lots in a helmet . . . ; the man whose lot first jumps out will take the worse [the second] portion" (1977, 24).

31. Jocasta's speech ends here.

34. they obeyed: The two sons obeyed their mother and Teiresias.

51. he: This could be Teiresias or, perhaps, Polyneikes mounting his horse to leave.

53–90. Teiresias' speech.

61–69. Too fragmentary to translate.

74. destined: Teiresias foretells Polyneikes' destiny: he will marry the daughter of King Adrastos of Argos.

85. Teiresias predicts disaster if one of the brothers breaks the agreement.

92–103. Polyneikes travels from Thebes south to "great-walled" Erythrai, crossing the Isthmos to Korinth, then to Kleonai and, finally, Argos.

SAPPHO

Sappho, a native of Mytilene on the island of Lesbos, composed lyric poetry in her local Aeolic dialect in the late seventh century. As an aristocratic woman, she would have married and may have had a daughter (Kleis).

Modern notions of the exclusivity of homosexuality and heterosexuality do not apply to the ancient world. Attractions between women did not interfere with the patriarchal structure, and may have been considered a normal aspect of female society. While the men of Lesbos engaged in political activities, aristocratic women, especially before marriage, had opportunities to form other alliances. Sappho's writing includes epithalamia (wedding songs) and poems that explore female desire and homoerotic friendship. Marriage was an occasion of joy as well as of sadness over the loss of friends and the change of life. Some of her writing reflects issues of loss, such as the sorrow of parting (probably due to the marriage of the loved one) and the remembrance of shared joy, as in 14 and 15. The poems are passionate and skillfully crafted; they show Sappho's awareness of the poet's function in her society.

Sappho's work was highly regarded in her own time and throughout antiquity. Of the nine books of her poetry collected in the Alexandrian period, only one definitely complete poem survives (1). The rest are from quotations by ancient grammarians, and from papyri, parchment, and one potsherd. The commentary below notes the material each fragment was discovered on, if other than a quotation.

Sappho 1: Voigt 1

Sappho uses a traditional prayer formula. The speaker invokes Aphrodite, reminding her of her previous epiphanies. Yet as the past tense verbs (lines 6–15) abruptly shift to present tense (line 16), Aphrodite seems to arrive and speak to Sappho directly once again. The speaker's present desire recalls Aphrodite's past action, which in turn results in Aphrodite's present promise of future satisfaction. The conclusion returns to the speaker's request for fulfillment, but her prayer has already been answered.

1. Immortal: The same word is translated as "unaging" in line 14.

10. sparrows: These birds are a symbol of fecundity.

18–24. The speaker quotes Aphrodite's words to her on previous occasions, but it is as if Aphrodite were addressing her at the present.

18. Again: The word, also in lines 16 and 25, refers to the recurring situation posited in the poem, in which the speaker desires a reluctant beloved and recalls that Aphrodite helped turn the situation around before.

19. back into the harness: In the manuscript, "back" is illegible, but possible. The standard interpretation is "to lead back to your love" (*s' agēn*), but I prefer the more descriptive "harness" (*sagēn*).

21–24. Aphrodite will make the other woman love Sappho as Sappho now loves her. The passage does not mean that the speaker will lose interest when the other woman pursues. The speaker wishes for reciprocal, mutual attraction. Aphrodite promises that, but by means of the goddess' own particular powers of "persuasion": "even against her will." The suggestion of the lover conquering the beloved is stronger here than elsewhere in Sappho's poetry, and closer to the archaic poetry by men.

her will: The Greek feminine participle *etheloisa* is the only direct evidence that the female speaker desires another female. The verbs in lines 21–23 do not indicate gender, and there are no separate personal pronouns.

28. ally: "Companion in battle, comrade in arms."

Sappho 2: Voigt 2 (potsherd)

This incantation draws the listeners into Aphrodite's sacred grove. The sound of the poem echoes the sense, eliciting the kind of trance-like spell that the poetry describes.

2. apple grove: "Lovely apple grove."

5. ripples: A "loud, clear sound."

7. murmuring: A "shimmering" or "rustling" movement.

8. deep sleep: A *kōma* is a trance-like sleep, associated with sexuality and trickery, induced by supernatural forces.

13. Kypris: A frequently used title of Aphrodite. The speaker asks Aphrodite herself to pour the nectar like wine. In Voigt's edition "pour" is a participle (the speaker states that Kypris is pouring), while in earlier editions it is an imperative (the speaker asks Kypris to pour).

Sappho 3: Voigt 17 (papyrus)

The trinity of Hera, Zeus, and Dionysos (Thyone/Semele's son), was worshiped on Lesbos. The poem calls for Hera to appear and answer the speaker's prayer, as she did in the past for the Atreidai kings (Agamemnon and Menelaos).

5–10. After Agamemnon and Menelaos accomplished great things at Troy, they came to Lesbos. Until the trinity answered their prayer, however, the kings were prevented from accomplishing some task, perhaps from leaving the island.

11. now: The speaker returns to the immediate request.

Sappho 4: Voigt 16 (papyrus)

Sappho here uses myth to illustrate her argument that "whatever one loves" appears most desirable. Helen left Menelaos to sail to Troy with Paris. Sappho composed songs of desire for an individual and for relationships between people rather than songs of battles and war. The absence of the beloved, "Anaktoria being gone," acts as Sappho's Muse here and in 14 and 15. The poem seems to end at line 20, although the papyrus indicates that twelve more lines followed.

3. fairest: "Most beautiful."

4. whatever: The line reads not "whomever" but "that thing, whatever it is" (neuter).

8. best man: Menelaos.

10. child: Hermione.

20. shining bronze: "Armor."

Sappho 5: Voigt 81

The Graces prefer those who wear garlands of flowers.

3. flowerful: "Things rich with flowers."

Sappho 6: Voigt 39

Sappho 7: Voigt 34

Stars are difficult to see during the full moon. Perhaps this poem refers to a beautiful woman who outshines even other beautiful women.

Sappho 8: Voigt 31

The speaker tells a woman how excited she gets at the mere sight of her, so that being close in conversation with her would be overwhelming.

2. that man: "That man" refers to anyone fortunate enough to be near her, not a specific man. The poem focuses on the desire that the addressee stimulates in the speaker, rather than the man—or even the desired woman.

9. delicate: "Slender, subtle."

11. cold: The text is corrupt here; some editors, including Voigt, omit "cold."

13. greener than grass: The word for "greener" in Greek can denote "fresh, moist, wet"—and can modify all the liquids of life, such as tears, blood, dew, and sap. Grass often has sexual connotations in archaic lyric. While "moister than grass" is perhaps more exact, it lacks Sappho's subtle eroticism. This image continues the listing of symptoms of erotic excitement. The speaker is full of life and close to death (line 15).

Sappho 9: Voigt 22 (papyrus)

The speaker may be addressing Gongyla; her name is possible in the second line of the Greek manuscript.

Sappho 10: Voigt 23 (papyrus)

The speaker likens one woman (line 3) to Helen's daughter Hermione (line 4), but not to Helen herself (line 5) since Helen is an immortal.

7. these: "These women."

Sappho 11: Voigt 33

Sappho 12: Voigt 56

1. woman: The Greek word is *parthenos*, a young marriageable woman, also translated as "virgin" or "maiden."

skill: The Greek *sophia* probably means "skill in poetry," although it could mean "wisdom."

Sappho 13: Voigt 41

1. beautiful ones: "Beautiful women" (feminine adjective).

Sappho 14: Voigt 94 (parchment)

This poem about the departure of a friend recalls their time together.

1. This line is most likely by the same speaker as in lines 4–5.

10. we shared: The verb for "experience" or "suffer" is used here and at line 4 with the two different connotations reflecting the two speakers.

18. anointed: Perhaps "anointed like a queen."

20. quenched: "Expelled your desire by satisfying it."

Sappho 15: Voigt 96 (parchment)

The speaker recalls an absent woman to comfort her friend.

4. you: Atthis (line 16).

undisguised: "Easily recognized."

8–9. The light from the moon connects the two women even across the barrier of sea and field.

11. flowering fields: The light illuminates blooming flowers and dew; both images have sexual connotations.

15. remembers: Memory, like the moonlight, unites the women.

17. She is consumed by thoughts of Atthis.

Sappho 16: Voigt 130 (a)

1. loosener of limbs: See note to Archilochos 19, line 1.

Sappho 17: Voigt 95 (parchment)
4. Hermes: He is the guide to the underworld.
9–10. lotus-shaded: The banks of the river to Hades are pictured as "covered with lotus-trees."

Sappho 18: Voigt 102
2. overwhelmed: "Conquered."
3. longing: Erotic desire.
boy: The word here is the regular Greek word for child, *pais*, which could be male or female.

Sappho 19: Voigt 47

Sappho 20: Voigt 146
Each word in the Greek line begins with *m*.

Sappho 21: Voigt 52

Sappho 22: Voigt 54

Sappho 23: Voigt 166
Sappho here tells a different version of Helen's birth, in which Leda is not raped by Zeus in the form of a swan, but instead finds an egg hidden in a fragrant flower.

Sappho 24: Voigt 48
1. I felt for you: The verb is a combination of physically seeking and wanting, touch and desire together.

Sappho 25: Voigt 126
1. companion: "Female friend."

Sappho 26: Voigt 63 (papyrus)
The poem addresses the god Dream.

Sappho 27: Voigt 168 (b)

Sappho 28: Voigt 121
The friend is male, the speaker female.

Sappho 29: Voigt 58 (papyrus)

5–8. old age: These lines speak of the signs of growing old: skin changing, hair turning white, and joints stiffening.

10. Perhaps "impossible to be unaging."

11. Dawn: Lines 11–14, and possibly the following two lines, refer to the goddess Dawn, who requested immortality for her human lover Tithonos but forgot to ask that he also remain unaging.

17–18. Passion for . . . life: These two lines seem to recall the first four lines of the fragment—perhaps passion (*eros*) for living transcends age.

light of life: Literally the Greek word is "sun"; Nagy (1990, 261) suggests that the poem may have contained the myth of Phaethon/Phaon, the son of the Sun.

Sappho 30: Voigt 42

The passage in which this fragment is quoted states that the poem refers to pigeons.

Sappho 31: Voigt 101(a)

This fragment refers to the sound of cicadas, perhaps in the heat of summer.

Sappho 32: Voigt 106

Sappho 33: Voigt 55

This is an invective against someone who does not share the Muses' gift of poetry. She was a nonentity in life and once she has died, she will remain unknown among the "obscure" dead.

3. Pierian: Pieria is the traditional home of the Muses.

Sappho 34: Voigt 57

Sappho 35: Voigt 49

These lines may not have been consecutive.

Sappho 36: Voigt 130 (b)

Sappho 37: Voigt 71 (papyrus)

3. Penthilian: The ruler Pittakos married into the house of Penthilos, which was among Alkaios' faction's rivals.

Sappho 38: Voigt 15 (papyrus)

Sappho 39: Voigt 158

Sappho 40: Voigt 37

Sappho 41: Voigt 50

Sappho 42: Voigt 137

Sappho 43: Voigt 120

Sappho 44: Voigt 5 (papyrus)
In this prayer, the speaker asks that her brother's wishes be fulfilled (lines 3–4), and that his wish be to "honor" or "respect" her (lines 9–10).
5. release: "Release" has the sense of "set free" to start over, or perhaps "amend."
6–7. The traditional heroic sentiment is to help your friends and hurt your enemies.
13. millet seed: Perhaps "small as a millet seed."

Sappho 45: Voigt 132
2. Kleis: Kleis is thought to be the name of Sappho's mother and daughter.

Sappho 46: Voigt 98 (a) and (b) (papyrus)
Sections (a) and (b) are from the same poem but not directly consecutive.
(a) The speaker states that her mother said that a purple hairband is most becoming for dark hair and fresh flowers for blonds.
1. Mother: Perhaps "said."
(b) 3. Although a gap follows this line, the remaining lines are probably from the same poem.
7. exile: Perhaps luxuries such as the colorful hairbands are not available in exile; Sappho was said to have been exiled from Mytilene.
8. Kleanax's sons: This was Myrsilos' family, another aristocratic faction in Mytilene.

Sappho 47: Voigt 104 (a)
1. Evening star: Hesperos.
gathers: The verb for "brings/gathers" is repeated four times in the poem for an incantational effect.

Sappho 48: Voigt 105 (a)

This is a poem about desire; some scholars say "the sweet apple" represents virginity or a bride. Sappho uses a technique of modifying statements: the second line says the pickers missed the apple, the third line corrects that—they wanted to pick it but could not reach (touch) it.

Sappho 49: Voigt 105 (b)

Unobservant men trample on delicate beauty; this poem may also refer to virginity.

Sappho 50: Voigt 44A (a) and (b) (papyrus)

Sections (a) and (b) are separate columns on the papyrus; they probably are from the same poem.

(a) The fragment opens with the children of Leto and Zeus, Phoibos Apollo and Artemis.

3–6. Artemis requests that Zeus allow her to remain a virgin and to roam the mountains.

7. father: Zeus grants her request.

8. Huntress: Artemis.

10. love: Eros never approaches the virgin goddess.

Sappho 51: Voigt 44 (papyrus)

This poem is about the marriage of Hektor and Andromache; it makes extensive use of epic phrases (formulas). The use of epic formulas lends an appropriate tone of antiquity to the story. A herald announces the arrival of Hektor and his bride Andromache (lines 4–10); the Trojans go to meet his ships (lines 11–19); and then the marriage procession escorts the bride and groom back to Troy (lines 20–33). An unknown number of lines are missing after line 19, from the center of this fragment.

2. Idaios: He is a Trojan herald.

11. father: Priam.

33. Paion: Apollo.

Sappho 52: Voigt 141

Since libations and prayers are usually made by mortals to the gods, the new couple must either be divine, partly divine, or particularly honored.

Sappho 53: Voigt 27 (papyrus)
Poems 53–59 are marriage songs (epithalamia); much of the language is repetitive or ritualistic.

Sappho 54: Voigt 112

Sappho 55: Voigt 113

Sappho 56: Voigt 115

Sappho 57: Voigt 111
This song jests that the bridegroom is so big that the carpenters will need to "raise the roof" for him to enter.
2. Hymen: Hymen is the god of marriage.
5. like Ares: This could mean the bridegroom approaches: impetuously, rapidly, like a warrior, or perhaps like Ares on his way to commit adultery with Aphrodite—extremely virile.
7. much bigger: This may be a phallic jest.

Sappho 58: Voigt 110
The "doorkeeper" guards the bridegroom's door, preventing other people from entering. Perhaps the bride's friends playfully taunt him with this song.

Sappho 59: Voigt 114

Sappho 60: Voigt 107

Sappho 61: Voigt 30 (papyrus)

Sappho 62: Voigt 154

Sappho 63: Voigt 140
This fragment is entirely alliterated in Greek: two words begin with a *t* sound, two with an *ah*, and the rest with a *k* sound.
1. The women ask Aphrodite what to do as her young lover Adonis dies anew each year at the festival of Adonis.
2. Aphrodite responds that they should ritually mourn.

Sappho 64: Voigt 150
1. those who serve the Muses: Poets.

Sappho 65: Voigt 51

  1. what I should do: This could mean "what I should set down," in regard to composing poetry.

Sappho 66: Voigt 160

  2. companions: "Female friends."

Sappho 67: Voigt 118

Sappho 68: Voigt 147

ALKAIOS

Alkaios, Sappho's contemporary in Mytilene on Lesbos, wrote in the local Aeolic dialect. Alkaios was a member of a noble family who lost the competition for political power in Mytilene against the first ruler on Lesbos, Melanchros, and then against Myrsilos. Pittakos initially joined with Alkaios against Myrsilos, but then switched his alliance. Alkaios attacked the leaders of the ruling parties, Myrsilos and then Pittakos, in his poems and presumably by more active means as well. He was exiled three times from Mytilene, but Pittakos eventually allowed him to return. After generations of aristocratic factions struggling for control and causing civil strife, the people of Mytilene accepted Pittakos' benevolent and peaceful rule. Pittakos ruled for ten years and then resigned; he later was considered one of the Seven Sages.

  Alkaios uses myth and metaphor for political persuasion. Poems that seem strictly mythological may have been part of his large percentage of political poems, but lacking the complete poem or the context of its performance, we cannot be certain.

  Poems 2–7 were discovered on papyri, 8 is from a quotation, and 1 is a quotation completed by papyrus.

Alkaios 1: Voigt 208

  1. conflict: The word *stasis* glosses as both (a) the position of the winds, the direction the winds come from, and (b) political strife, faction, and civil war. *Stasis* functions both as a description of a storm wrecking a ship and as a metaphor of the ship of state attacked by internal dissent.

  9. halyards: The manuscript's "anchors" does not make sense for a ship at

sea, unless the ship was in shallow water. It appears likely that the word for some kind of rope was replaced in the copying of the original manuscript.

12. stay: Perhaps "both feet stay" tangled or caught.

14. cargo: Perhaps the "cargo" is carried off.

Alkaios 2: Voigt 130 (b)

Alkaios details what his exile from Mytilene means: he has been driven away from his traditional political rights—of meeting in assembly and council—and he is isolated from the aristocratic companions of his political faction.

11. conflict: Alkaios resists giving up the *stasis* which was the cause of his exile.

15. women: That he has nothing better to do than watch the women celebrate their rituals emphasizes the isolation from his male political cohorts.

16–20. The beauty contest and annual women's ritual are seen from an outsider's perspective. In Sappho's poems, women's celebrations are portrayed from the participants' or insiders' view.

21–22. gods: Perhaps the line read, "when will the Olympian gods release me?"

Alkaios 3: Voigt 298

Poem 3 details Athena's vengeance against Ajax and his men after Ajax raped Kassandra in Athena's sanctuary during the sack of Troy. Clues in the fragment suggest that the poem warns the people against supporting Pittakos, Alkaios' rival and the ruler of the city. Ajax's men suffered because they did nothing to punish the criminal; so, Alkaios implies, the people of Mytilene will suffer if they continue to support Pittakos.

3. stoning: Death by stoning probably is meant here.

4. Achaians: The Greeks.

5. killed: If the Achaians had killed Ajax after his transgression, then they would have sailed safely home instead of being wrecked at sea.

7. sea: Perhaps "they'd have found the sea calm."

8–11. Priam's daughter: Kassandra clasped the chin of a statue of Athena in supplication while the Greeks attacked Troy.

12. Daiphobos: Kassandra's brother was killed.

16–19. Kassandra's and Pallas Athena's chastity contrasts with Ajax's sexual violence. Athena's rage, however, is more deadly than Ajax's—she is "rich in warspoils" and the "giver of war."

22. Lokrian: Ajax.

23. daughter of Zeus: Athena.

Alkaios 4: Voigt 34

The poem invokes the Dioscuri, Kastor and Polydeukes, who rescue men at sea. They were thought to show themselves in the electrical discharge, known as St. Elmo's fire, that sometimes dances about ship masts. The final three stanzas of the poem are missing.

Alkaios 5: Voigt 42

The poem contrasts Helen and Thetis, blaming Helen for the destruction of Troy, not Thetis' son Achilles, who destroyed both the city and himself.

1–4. Bitter troubles came for Priam and Troy because of Helen.

5. son of Aiakos: Peleus and Thetis had a proper wedding with the approval of the gods, unlike Helen's elopement with Paris.

7. Nereus: Thetis is the daughter of the sea-god Nereus.

9. Cheiron: He is the centaur who tutored Achilles.

13. child: Achilles.

14. tawny: This word often is used of Helen ("goldenhaired"), and also is the name of one of Achilles' immortal horses (Xanthos).

15. those: The Trojans.

Alkaios 6: Voigt 283

This poem also condemns Helen for leaving her husband Menelaos and causing the Trojan War.

2. man: Paris made Helen mad with passion.

3. traitorous guest: "Deceiver of his host."

8. daughter: Helen.

10. brothers: According to Homer, twelve of Paris' brothers were killed.

Alkaios 7: Voigt 38 (a)

Since no one returns from death, one should enjoy life now. Even Sisyphos, who escaped death once, had to die eventually.

5. Sisyphos: He tricked Death once to allow him to return from the underworld and then stayed until he died a natural death. The second, and final, time that he crossed the river Acheron to Hades, Zeus condemned him to continually push a boulder to the top of a hill.

12. The poem might end here even though part of another line is visible ("north wind").

Alkaios 8: Voigt 347

This drinking song is a lyrical version of Hesiod's passage (582–88) in *Works and Days*.

1. dogstar: The star Sirius, associated with heat, pestilence, and destruction, rises above the horizon in the heat of the "dog days."

6. Weak: "Delicate."

IBYKOS

Ibykos lived in the second half of the sixth century. He was born at Rhegium in Italy, but left there for the court of Polykrates, the ruler of Samos. Ibykos wrote narrative poetry, presumably choral lyric, in the same literary language as Stesichoros—epic language mixed with the Doric dialect conventional in choral song. His erotic poetry, however, bears closer resemblance to the solo lyric of Sappho and Anakreon than to Stesichoros' poetry. Poems 1–4 are from quotations, 5 from a papyrus.

Ibykos 1: PMG 286

Ibykos contrasts the peaceful and orderly season of Spring with the speaker's violent, uncontrolled passion. The garden is a cultivated version of Aphrodite's apple grove in Sappho 2. In Sappho's poem the speaker is in the garden, caught in its spell, while here the speaker is outside, separate from the garden's peace that contrasts with his own situation.

2. irrigated: The garden is irrigated by channels from a river, an image that contrasts with the "parching madness" in line 11.

3. Virgins: They may be nymphs of some sort. While their "inviolate garden" is undefiled by shameless, incessant sexuality, it is not devoid of sexuality altogether: the quince trees and vinebuds flower, and quinces ("Kydonian apples") are associated with the new growth of love.

6–7. Love: For the speaker, eros has no season of growth or rest, but flares up constantly. "Rests" literally means "in bed."

9. Boreas: The wild and stormy north wind. This love-wind comes from Aphrodite.

10. Kypris: Aphrodite.

12. shakes: The manuscript has "guards/ambushes" (*phylassei*), which makes little sense in this context (although the idea of hidden menace is attractive).

Ibykos 2: PMG 287

1. Eros arrives through the eyes of the beloved, who looks at the lover in a way that makes him melt with desire.

4. infinite nets: Aphrodite's "nets from which one cannot escape."

5–9. The speaker has come victorious from the love contest many times before, but now, as he nears old age, he says he goes into it only under duress. It seems that he is only pretending to be reluctant, but really is confident of another victory.

Ibykos 3: PMG 317 (a)

3. purple birds: These birds, perhaps purple gallinules, have secretive habits and feed at night.

4. halcyons: They are mythical sea-birds.

Ibykos 4: PMG 285

1. Herakles killed the Molione, Siamese twins joined at the trunk.

2. white horses: They may be called "white-horsed boys" because their father, Poseidon, is associated with horses (and the whitecaps of waves).

Ibykos 5: SLG 151

This poem is humorous and delightfully extravagant in language and use of epic diction. The exaggerated and overabundant echoes of epic phrases go beyond homage. The poem recalls and demonstrates the power of song, as Barron amply shows: "The 'formulae' are in inverted commas. . . . [the heroes] are immortal precisely because of the poetry written about them and for no other reason" (135). The "lasting fame" of heroes and contemporary famous men, such as Polykrates, depends upon poetry good enough to be remembered.

In addition to emphasizing the power of song to immortalize its subjects, Ibykos uses epic formulaic diction in order to parody epic. Note the condensation of the Trojan War, the multiple epithets where one would do (lines 20–22), and the tricky way of quickly mentioning topics that the poet says he is not going to mention (lines 10–22).

The poem has the triadic structure characteristic of much choral poetry (see introductory note on Stesichoros). Each triad of strophe, antistrophe, and epode expresses a complete thought; our text begins with an antistrophe.

1–3. The Greeks left their home territories ("Argos") to conquer King Priam's city of Troy.

6. blond: I usually translate *xanthos* as "tawny" for horses and "golden-haired" for people, but here I echo Ibykos' contrast with *chrysos* in line 9—Aphrodite's truly "gold" hair. Helen's appearance stimulated the war that Zeus planned and that Aphrodite caused.

8. Pergamon: The citadel of Troy.

10–22. The poet lists what he does not want to sing about, what he will pass over without telling in full. Each Homeric phrase conjures up part of the story, then the poet moves on to the next part as a non-topic for his song.

16. surpassing: Only here before Plato is *hyperaphanon* used in a positive sense. Usually it means "arrogant/overweening." Perhaps here too the word has some negative connotations—"arrogant manliness (*aretē*)."

20–22. This is an exaggerated description of Agamemnon, the leader of the whole expedition that caused so much grief. Ibykos combines two versions of Agamemnon's lineage: in Homer, Agamemnon is the son of Atreus; in Hesiod's *Catalogue of Women* he is the son of Pleisthenes, who is the son of Atreus.

25–26. The papyrus shows that one word is missing in these two lines, but with that word there would be one word too many for the line. Since the lines make sense as they are, most people assume that the missing word was added later as a gloss. Barron (128), however, believes that "mortal" is intrusive, a gloss for the unusual word for "living" (*dieros*, "active, vigorous, alive"). He argues that the missing word would be "unaided": no living man could tell all the details unaided or untaught by the Muses.

On the other hand, the double adjectives match the style and tone of the rest of the poem: not just a man, but a *mortal* man, and a *living* mortal man. No mortal man, alive now, could tell the whole story, each and all the things severally. Homer "told all" in epic, but a lyric poet does not tell all the details, even in his narrative poetry.

32. Ibykos lists the best Greeks (Achaians) in war and then (lines 36–46) the best in regard to beauty.

37. Kyanippos: A little-known figure in Greek myth, from the second generation of young heroes who arrived in time to sack Troy (Ilion).

41. Hyllis: The mother of Zeuxippos, who was king of Sikyon at the time of the Trojan War.

41–45. The Trojans and the Greeks (Danaans) found Troilos, one of Priam's sons, and Zeuxippos equal in beauty, just as gold and orichalcum are precious and have the same beauty to the eye. Orichalcum is brass or the yellow mountain copper used to make brass.

46. these: All the beautiful young men listed in the last triad.

47–48. undying fame: *Kleos* is the fame conferred by song on heroic deeds, and the medium of song that confers the fame. According to Nagy, Ibykos is saying, "my *kleos* will be your *kleos*, because my song of praise for you will be your means to fame. Conversely, since you merit permanent fame, my song praising you will be permanent, and consequently I the Singer will have permanent fame as well" (1974, 251).

ANAKREON

In the second half of the sixth century, Anakreon wrote monody, in an Ionic dialect, primarily on the themes of love and wine. He was born in Teos in Asia Minor, entertained at Polykrates' court in Samos, and later spent time in Athens. The elegance and charm of his poetry inspired lasting admiration. We have about sixty lyric poems composed by various authors in imitation of Anakreon between c. 200 B.C.E. and c. 500 C.E. Poems 1–10 are from quotations and 11 was discovered on papyrus.

Anakreon 1: PMG 356 (a) and (b)

The first stanza calls for heavy drinking; the second stanza, which is probably not directly sequential, suggests tapering off into more moderate drinking.

(a) 3. long draught: "Without stopping for breath or closing one's mouth."

4. The Greeks mixed their wine with water.

6. tastefully: I translate *anubristōs* ("decorously"), instead of the manuscript's *an hubristōs* ("insultingly").

(b) 4. Scythian drinking: "Excessive, raucous drinking."

Anakreon 2: PMG 348

Anakreon 3: PMG 357

    1. Lord: Dionysos.

    9. counsellor: Anakreon puns on "counsellor" (*sumboulos*) and the boy's name, Kleoboulos, "famous counsellor."

Anakreon 4: PMG 358

Eros calls the speaker to play with a certain girl; she rejects him ostensibly because he is too old, but actually because she is interested in another female instead.

    5. well-founded: An epic word meaning "good to live in" or "well-built."

    6–7. The Greek word order adds information that qualifies the previous information one step at a time: "on the one hand, my hair, since it's white, she finds fault with, on the other hand . . ."

    8. another girl: The surprise ending is a humorous revelation of the girl's sexual preference.

        The ending of the poem is open to numerous other interpretations because of the ambiguity of the Greek. "Another girl" (*allēn*) means "another" someone or something of feminine gender. While I interpret the Greek in a common grammatical way, as referring to another female person, there are other possibilities (see Dover 183). Since "hair" is feminine in Greek, "another" could modify "hair"; the girl may be eyeing another man's hair, presumably that of a younger man. It could also mean that she is staring open-mouthed at a man's pubic hair, as some scholars have suggested, in preparation for fellatio. The reference to Lesbos is not a deciding factor because women from Lesbos, by a few centuries after Sappho's time, were ridiculed in comedy with non–gender-exclusive hypersexuality. On the other hand, Sappho's poetry describes a world of female homoerotic attractions, which the mention of Lesbos certainly recalls. In addition, there are two possible references to Sappho's poetry: Sappho uses the word "fancy" (*poikilos*, elsewhere translated as "many-hued/colored," see Sappho 6) eight times in her extant poetry, and her fragments exhibit a similar technique of qualifying in successive phrases (see Sappho 48). Of course, Anakreon may have made the poem deliberately ambiguous to amuse his symposium listeners.

Anakreon 5: PMG 360

    1. virgin: "Virgin girl."

Anakreon 6: PMG 376

Leukadian Rock: The Leukadian (White) Rock is a "Lovers' Leap"—lovers jump from the rock to get over their lovesickness. See Nagy (1990) for a fascinating discussion.

Anakreon 7: PMG 398

Anakreon 8: PMG 413

Anakreon 9: PMG 417

The female as a horse to be tamed provides a common image of male domination. The "filly" here ignores the narrator's threat. See Winkler (1990) on competition and male domination in Greek culture. The man threatens conquest because he himself is conquered by Eros; he displaces his helpless state onto the desired woman.

3. stubbornly: "Pitilessly."

11–12. "Since you've no skillful rider experienced in horses."

Anakreon 10: PMG 395

Anakreon 11: PMG 346

With so much of this fragment missing it is difficult to get at the sense. It is possible that the speaker claims Herotima acts like a fearful child around her mother, who protectively rears her, but Herotima has already entered Aphrodite's fields and "been around." It also is possible that line 13 is the beginning of a different poem.

3. child: Herotima.

4. she: Perhaps "she" is Herotima's mother.

13. tramp: The Greek *leōphore* literally means "bearing people," as a thoroughfare, but is used for "whore."

SIMONIDES

Simonides (c. 556–468) was born on Keos, an island near the southeastern tip of Attika, and wrote primarily in the Ionic dialect. He practiced his poetic trade throughout the Greek world: in Hipparchos' Athens, at the courts of the Aleuadai and Skopadai in Thessaly, and then in Sicily (c. 476) for Hieron of Syracuse. Simonides may have invented epinikian odes for winners in the athletic games. He was famous for his skillful lyric and elegiac poetry; it is difficult to determine which of these particular poems are choral. All of the poems survive in quotations, except for 6 on a papyrus.

Simonides 1: PMG 520
   4. Death is the destiny of all human beings alike.

Simonides 2: PMG 521
   Human fortune changes faster than the erratic movement of a dragonfly.
   3. changing course: *Metastasis* means a change of position or direction, a counterrevolution, an overturn of fortune.
   4. dragonfly: The "longwinged fly" is probably a dragonfly or bluebottle fly.

Simonides 3: PMG 522
   All things in life result in the same end.
   1. Charybdis: She is the whirlpool monster that sucks men down to their deaths.
   2. heroic excellence: "Great *aretai*" (excellences) are brave or heroic deeds, or anything that shows "excellences."

Simonides 4: PMG 531
   The battle at Thermopylai in the war between Persia and Greece in 480 left a troop of Spartan soldiers and their commander, Leonidas, dead. The Spartans chose to remain and fight to the death against a far greater Persian force in order to delay the Persian invasion. They were able to inflict high casualties and held the pass until they were betrayed by a Greek who showed the Persians a way around. The Spartan dead were buried at Thermopylai and honored as heroes.
   Podlecki provides a thorough discussion of this poem. He interprets "glorious fortune" (*euklees ha tucha*, line 2) as "chance brought fame" (191), that the chance of being at the right place at the right time brought an opportunity to win *kleos* (fame).
   3. While usually the dead are lamented at the gravesite, the dead at Thermopylai are worshiped as heroes, remembered and praised for their bravery.
   4. shroud: The shroud is the praise and honor that they are wrapped in, which will not deteriorate with time.

6. acclaim: The "good repute" of Greece, which the soldiers won, now attends or inhabits their burial place.

7–9. Leonidas is the prime example of the soldiers; he won "everlasting fame" through his courage and *aretē* (excellence or manliness).

Simonides 5: PMG 581

Kleoboulos, who ruled over Lindos in Rhodes (c. 600), was considered one of the Seven Sages. He wrote an epitaph on Midas claiming that a bronze grave marker would last as long as all things in nature, listing the same sorts of things as Simonides does. Simonides' poem says that only a fool would claim a man-made object could withstand the powers of nature.

7. counsel: This is a pun on Kleoboulos' name, which means "famous counsel."

Simonides 6: PMG 541

It is difficult to be good, but the ones who are good cannot be tarnished by the base.

2–3. a mouth without a door: The words of someone who speaks incessantly, never closing his mouth, are like smoke, which quickly dissipates.

4–5. Slander doesn't stain the good man because truth is all-powerful.

7–11. Desires for profit, or love and conquest, "force" a man away from good and lawful actions.

9. Aphrodite: A short fragment from another poem by Simonides connects Aphrodite and the war-god Ares: Love is the "cruel child of wily Aphrodite, whom she bore to crafty Ares" (PMG 575).

Simonides 7: PMG 542

This poem survives as Plato quotes it in his *Protagoras*. Plato says the poem is addressed to Skopas, the prince of Thessaly. Simonides says that when Pittakos said it is hard to be good, he didn't go far enough. It is *impossible* to be good unless one also always has good fortune, which is the lot of gods, not humans. Circumstance helps determine whether a man is good or bad. Therefore the best man is one who does nothing shameful by choice. Gentili (66–71) has an interesting discussion of Plato's use of this poem.

3. foursquare: To be "foursquare" is to be perfect according to the Pythagorean ideal. The perfect man is traditionally strong in body, mind, wealth, and birth.

4–10. Plato omitted these lines.

11. Pittakos: Pittakos, the tyrant of Mytilene, was considered a sage (although not by Alkaios).

17. fares well: As long as a man has good fortune he can be a good man.

19–20. This is Plato's paraphrase of Simonides' lines.

27–30. Since no human is wholly blameless, everyone who does nothing shameful of his own free will—a morally good man—deserves praise.

33–34. Plato's paraphrase.

39. fair: "Beautiful, good, noble."

Simonides 8: PMG 584

4. her: Pleasure.

Simonides 9: PMG 508

"Halcyon days," named after the legendary sea-bird, are calm, windless days in the midst of a usually stormy month.

Simonides 10: PMG 543

The myth referred to here is the story of Danaë and her son Perseus. It was foretold that Danaë's son would kill her father, Akrisios. Akrisios locked her in a tower to prevent her from marrying, but Zeus, in a shower of gold, impregnated Danaë. When her father found that she had given birth to a son, he locked mother and son in a chest and set it out to sea. Most of this fragment consists of Danaë speaking to her sleeping baby as they drift on the water.

1–3. Within the chest, Danaë is tossed about.

4. cheeks wet with tears: With Simonides' characteristic use of negatives (see Carson 1988), the phrase literally is "with not unwet cheeks."

9. boat: Danaë refers to the chest as a boat.

10. gleaming: The line could also be read "in gleaming night," in which the night, rather than the boat, shines.

11. stretched out: The baby is stretched out in the chest.

16. fair face: This phrase could be "baby with the lovely face," or the line may be missing the verb "show." Only Perseus' face is uncovered.

18–19. "You would hold [i.e. turn] your little ear under [i.e. to] my words."

23. Father Zeus: The traditional epithet has added effect when Danaë asks Zeus to help his own son.

Simonides 11: PMG 553

Simonides 12: PMG 595
    No wind prevented Orpheus' song from being heard.

Simonides 13: PMG 567

Simonides 14: PMG 579
    3. The text is corrupt here.
    5–7. Line 4 is followed by two examples of mortals to whom *Aretē* ("Excellence") is not visible.
    7. prowess: "Manliness."

KORINNA

Korinna lived in Tanagra, a town in Boiotia. She wrote lyric narratives on local Boiotian themes. Korinna was known for her original versions of myths—both of the longest fragments tell versions of the myths otherwise unknown. The papyrus fragments show that this text was not written until the third century, and Korinna is not mentioned until the first century. Because of this, some scholars place Korinna in the third century. However, the current trend is to accept the ancient testimony that she was a contemporary of Pindar in the fifth century. See Snyder (1989) for a summary of the evidence. Poems 1–3 and 15 survive on papyrus, 4–14 through quotations.

Korinna 1: PMG 655
    Korinna describes her art as reworking the old myths, the "father-songs" (*logia paterōn*, line 9), in her own way to delight her female audience in her hometown. As a popular poet ("the city delighted," line 4), Korinna assumes that her audience would be familiar with the song subjects she mentions.
    1. Terpsichore: She is the Muse of dance. This reference may imply that Korinna wrote choral lyric.
    2. old tales: The Greek *weroia* most likely means "narratives" and may not have the connotation of "old," but the following stanzas justify the sense.
    5. clear as the swallow's: This phrase in the Greek is one compound adjective modifying "voice" (*ligouro-kōtilus*); the precise meaning of the second half of the word is uncertain. It refers to some bird-like sound: "prattling," "coaxing," "plaintive," or "loud and lively" have been suggested. Simonides (PMG

586) has: "The much-*kōtiloi* nightingales, fresh-throated (birds) of spring." However, *kōtilos* is also a colloquial Boiotian word for the swallow, whose voice is *ligouros* (high, clear, sweet) and expressive.

9–11. The poet reworks ("in my own way") the old stories for her audience of women.

13. Kephisos: Kephisos is the name of an early Boiotian leader and of a Boiotian river.

14. Orion: He is a mythical Boiotian hunter and a constellation. The prophet Akraiphen (3, line 27) is one of his fifty sons.

15–16. strong: The adjective may modify Orion rather than his sons (although see 3, line 17): "and his fifty sons, whom the mighty man mingling with nymphs . . . " The poem may have continued with the story of the nymphs who bore Orion's sons.

Korinna 2: PMG 654 col. i 12–34

The story is of a singing contest between Kithairon and Helikon (Boiotian mountains). The fragment begins with the second song, which is generally considered to be the winning song by Kithairon.

The narrative then describes the voting process by the gods, the crowning of Kithairon, and Helikon's temper tantrum upon losing.

1–6. The song tells the story of the goddess Rhea hiding her infant son Zeus from his father Kronos, who had swallowed his earlier progeny. The semidivine Kouretes on Krete protected Zeus by making noise so Kronos couldn't hear him. The emphasis here is on Rhea, who won honor for saving her son.

19–22. Helikon, a mountain famous for its association with the Muses and Hesiod, here mutilates a mountain (and thereby creates his own "share" of stones; cf. line 11).

Korinna 3: PMG 654 col. iii 12–51

This poem tells the story of the river Asopos' nine daughters, who have been kidnapped by four gods. Asopos has come to ask the prophet Akraiphen about his daughters; the entire fragment, except for the last stanza, is Akraiphen's reply.

1–10. The four gods were convinced by the love deities to seize the girls. Zeus and Poseidon each took three, Apollo two, and Hermes one.

7. Kypris: Aphrodite.

11–14. Asopos' daughters will bear demigod sons and remain unaging themselves, gaining fame and immortality—the names of the nine daughters actually were the names of local islands and towns, including Korinna's Tanagra.

15–32. Akraiphen next provides his prophetic credentials to explain how he got this information.

15. oracular tripod: A prophet would sit on Apollo's bronze tripod to receive divine oracles.

16–17. Akraiphen is the only one of fifty brothers to have the gift of prophecy.

21–30. Apollo granted the ability to give prophecies (the "honor") first to Euonomos, second to Poseidon's son Hyrieus, third to Orion, and then to Orion's son, Akraiphen.

33–35. Akraiphen advises Asopos to accept that the gods have claimed his daughters, which makes Asopos "father-in-law of gods."

37–40. Asopos is relieved; the fragment breaks off before his reply.

Korinna 4: PMG 657
1. The speaker in the poem, more likely a goddess than a friend, addresses Korinna.

Korinna 5: PMG 658
1. happy: Usually this word is used of gods and translated "blessed."
2. Boiotos: He is the hero who gave his name to Boiotia.

Korinna 6: PMG 660

Korinna 7: PMG 662

Korinna 8: PMG 663

Korinna 9: PMG 664 (a)
Myrtis was a Boiotian poet who also wrote mythological narratives. She was believed to have taught Pindar and Korinna. None of her poetry survives. This tantalizing fragment lacks a context for accurate interpretation. Is the "I" the poet or a persona? This fragment may exhibit a tension concerning the role of a female poet, that perhaps female poets should only write a certain kind of poetry. Conversely, it may be a critique of Myrtis' portrayal of women (a prose paraphrase of one Myrtis poem tells of a woman who causes a man's death and her own suicide by falsely accusing him of rape). Or perhaps the criticism is simply that Myrtis competed with Pindar in his territory, i.e., wrote poetry too

much like Pindar's. Pindar was most famous for his epinikia of winners in the athletic games. See Korinna 10.

Korinna 10: PMG 664 (b)
   If 9 and 10 are part of one poem, perhaps Korinna blames Myrtis for not composing heroic narratives about the *aretē* (excellence) of women as Korinna does.

Korinna 11: PMG 666

Korinna 12: PMG 669
   Daughter of Hyria; Antiope was the daughter of Hyria and the river Asopos.

Korinna 13: PMG 674
   Thespia: Thespia, a town in south Boiotia near the foot of Mt. Helikon, attracted visitors to see its sanctuary of the Muses.

Korinna 14: PMG 678

Korinna 15: PMG 690
   Page's earlier edition (1953) accepts Korinna as the author, but his PMG (1962) expresses uncertainty. The title in the papyrus is "Orestes."

TELESILLA

Telesilla is famous for saving her city, Argos, from a siege by the Spartan army. After the Argive army was defeated by Spartan troops led by Kleomenes (c. 494), Telesilla rallied the remaining people in the city—old men, women, and slaves—to fight. They were able to defend the city until the Spartans withdrew.
   Telesilla wrote lyric poetry, addressed primarily to women, about Artemis and Apollo ("sun-loving," PMG 718). This single quotation is the only extant fragment longer than one word.

Telesilla 1: PMG 717
   The virgin goddess Artemis flees from the river god Alpheos. The more common version has Arethusa praying to Artemis to help her escape Alpheos who tries to rape her.

PRAXILLA

Praxilla wrote lyric poetry—hymns, dithyrambs, and drinking songs—in mid-fifth-century Sikyon (on the Gulf of Korinth). The poems survive in quotations.

Praxilla 1: PMG 747

In the ancient saying, "sillier than Praxilla's Adonis," Praxilla is scorned for putting the sun and cucumbers together. In her hymn, Adonis replies to the question in the underworld of what he misses most from the world above. Praxilla shows a practical understanding of human life and joy by setting the distant heavenly lights together with the immediate, crisp taste of earth's ripe fruit. The poem has certain verbal echoes of Sappho 4: fairest (line 3), radiant/shining, face (line 18).

3. cucumbers: The name of Praxilla's city, Sikyon, also is the word for "cucumber-bed."

Praxilla 2: PMG 748

This is part of a dithyramb addressed to Achilles.

Praxilla 3: PMG 749

Poems 3 and 4 are drinking songs.

1. Admetos: When Admetos was given the gift of avoiding his destined death if he could find someone to die for him, only his wife Alkestis was willing to.

Praxilla 4: PMG 750

Praxilla 5: PMG 754

2. The new bride still looks like the young virgin she was before marriage, but now she is a woman in "the things below."

ERINNA

Erinna wrote hexameter and elegiac poetry in the late fourth century, on an island off southwest Asia Minor (probably on Telos). Erinna's poetry was nearly as famous as Sappho's in antiquity. Erinna was believed to have died shortly after she wrote her masterpiece, poem 1, at nineteen years old. Although line 35 of this poem probably refers to Erinna as nineteen, there is no reason to assume that she actually was nineteen at the time of writing or that she died young. At least three of the six extant poems and fragments concern the death of a friend after marriage. The close connection between marriage and death is a traditional motif in Greek literature, which reflects emotional and physical realities. Death in childbirth was an ever-present possibility.

Poems 1–3 survived on papyrus, 4–6 in quotations.

Erinna 1: Supp. Hell. 401

Erinna's three hundred–line hexameter poem is a lament over the death of a childhood friend, Baukis, who died soon after marriage. The poem skillfully unites epic meter with a Sapphic theme (loss of a friend) and Sapphic Aeolicisms. It was known as the "Distaff," a title reflecting the recurrent imagery of weaving. Weaving is a metaphor for poetry writing and the "spinning" of the Fates (perhaps alluded to in line 39), as well as part of the child's game of tortoise-tag (perhaps in line 11) and the daily task for women of all ages and classes (lines 21, 37). See Arthur for a particularly illuminating discussion of tortoise and weaving symbolism.

The poem tells of Erinna's and Baukis' childhood together, recalling the games and innocent fears (lines 3–25), Baukis' marriage (lines 26–28), and Erinna's mourning mixed with fear of marriage and loneliness (lines 29–52). Erinna mingles present mourning with memories of the past and anxieties about the future.

3–15. These lines refer to a game like tag. One girl, the "tortoise," sits in the middle of a circle responding to the other children's questions. When they ask her what she is doing, she replies "weaving" (perhaps in line 11); to the question of how her child died, she answers, "from white horses he leapt into the sea." As she says this, the tortoise girl jumps up and tags another girl to become the tortoise. Here Baukis was the tortoise (line 13) who caught Erinna (line 14), who as the new tortoise chased Baukis (line 15).

16–18. The tortoise game is just a memory Erinna recalls in her grief over Baukis' death. The "traces" are memories of childhood games. The word "traces" may actually be the word for "games," partially obscured in the papyrus.

19–20. Some of the games they played were dolls or pretending to be brides.

20–22. In the mornings, Erinna's mother did something regarding weavers in their house. The girls spent their time together in one or the other's house.

23–25. Mormo (all Greek bogies are female) continually changes her appearance and eats children. The threat of Mormo scared them as children. These three lines on the bogy form the transition from memories of childhood. Mormo may represent a child's fear of maturity and sexuality, and the changes they bring to a woman's body.

26–28. Erinna first lost Baukis to marriage and then to death. Aphrodite caused Baukis to forget their long friendship (see Sappho 4). The "bed" Baukis got into could refer to the marriage bed with her husband, or to sharing a bed with the narrator before marriage (Snyder 1989, 95).

29–33. Since Erinna is unmarried and not related to Baukis, she is not allowed to mourn in the traditional manner—wailing with other women over the corpse, with her "hair unbound," raking her cheeks. Instead, she must mourn privately at home while she continues her weaving. "Shame," instead of her nails, may redden her cheeks because she cannot attend the funeral, prevented from seeing Baukis even dead.

35. Baukis died when Erinna was nineteen.

36. dear: Perhaps Erinna was a "dear" girl in her mother's house.

37–44. The imagery of weaving, virginity, and old age suggests contemplation of her fate. The Moirai (Fates) spin human destiny. Perhaps, "gazing on the distaff," she sees herself remaining unmarried, growing old now without her friend. Unmarried old women were seen as having special powers of influencing fertility "through the potency of their own unrealized fertility" (Arthur, 64).

45–52. This address to Baukis and the god of marriage, Hymen, implies that marriage is deadly and far more to be feared than their childhood bogy, Mormo. The "flame" could be the fire of wedding torches and/or a funeral pyre (see 5, line 5).

Erinna 2: Supp. Hell. 402

The lamentations of the living cannot penetrate the silent darkness of the underworld.

Erinna 3: Supp. Hell. 404

This highly alliterative fragment puns on the related words for "escort" and "send" (*pomp-*, *pemp-*). The fish, Pompilos, tends to swim alongside of ships. Hermes, known as the *Pempōn*, escorts the dead into the underworld.

2. friend: The friend could be the dead Baukis.

Erinna 4: Gow-Page 1

The dead Baukis addresses her funeral monument, a column with two sirens holding an urn. She tells the monument to inform passersby about her, and that it was Erinna who gave her a voice through the epigram itself. Thus Erinna speaks for Baukis, who asks the tomb to speak for her.

2. ashes: The urn would only symbolically contain ashes; the ashes from a cremation would be buried.

8. engraved: The epigram provides the illusion that it is a physical object, carved in stone.

Erinna 5: Giangrande 1

The Greek edition is the same as Gow-Page 2, but without the emendations in lines 5, 6, and 8. Giangrande demonstrates how the manuscript reading does not need the corrections generally accepted.

Here Baukis' tomb addresses potential readers of her grave inscription.

3. malicious: Death likes to take his victims young.

fine letters: The "beautiful sign" is the epigram itself.

5–8. The god of marriage, Hymen, rejoiced over the torches in the wedding procession, but then changed the wedding song to threnody with Baukis' death. Indeed, Baukis died so soon after marriage that her father-in-law lit her funeral pyre with fire from those same wedding torches.

Erinna 6: Gow-Page 3

The painter is likened to Prometheus, who fashioned humans from clay. The portrait of Agatharchis is only lacking a voice to be like the whole girl herself.

ANYTE

Anyte was an Arkadian poet (c. 300). Within the framework of inscriptional epigram, Anyte creatively developed new themes, such as animal epitaphs and pastoral. Her dialect was a blend of Ionic and Doric, perhaps influenced more by sound than location or convention. The Greek is full of rhyme, alliteration, and assonance. Anyte's epigrams were collected in the *Greek Anthology*.

Anyte 1: Geoghegan 1

The spear is propped up in Athena's temple as a dedication from Echekratidas, but the verbs "stand" and "rest" personify the spear.

1–2. The image here is of the spear in the battlefield set point upward, with blood from slain enemies dripping down around the butt ("talon") of the spear onto the ground.

Anyte 2: Geoghegan 2

Kleubotos of Tegea dedicated a large bowl, made by Aristoteles from Kleitor, to Athena.

Anyte 3: Geoghegan 3

1. Theudotos: In the Greek, his name is echoed in "placed gift" (*theto dōron*).

2. hair-raising Pan: Pan has bristling hair that stands on end and he makes people's hair stand on end as he causes "panic."

3. holy harvest: The harvest may have been of wine.

4. honeysweet: This is usually used for wine, not water.

Anyte 4: Geoghegan 19

The first two lines pose a question to Pan; Pan replies in the next two lines.

2. reed pipe: Pan-pipes.

4. fertile crops: The calves graze on all the rich herbage on the hillside—more likely wild crops than cultivated ones.

Anyte 5: Geoghegan 15

The oiled wooden statue of Aphrodite is set on a cliff overlooking the sea. The waves are afraid to act up within sight of her statue, so they provide smooth sailing.

1. Kypris: Aphrodite.

Anyte 6: Geoghegan 17

A statue of Hermes, guardian of the road, provides a resting spot and water for travellers.

Anyte 7: Geoghegan 16

1. luxuriant laurel: "The beautiful, luxuriant leaves of the laurel tree."

4. breath of Zephyros: Zephyros is the western breeze; the workers are urged to catch their breath while the breeze resuscitates them.

Anyte 8: Geoghegan 18

Anyte 9: Geoghegan 13

Children ride a goat around a temple. The children think they are in control since they have reined the goat, but reins and a noseband would have little effect if the goat weren't willing.

Anyte 10: Geoghegan 14

The goat, here associated with the god Dionysos, proudly eyes his thick beard.

Anyte 11: Geoghegan 12

This epitaph is in the voice of a dolphin who has been beached by waves onto the shore.

3. oarlocks: "Thole-pins."

4. figurehead: Ships often sported a dolphin figurehead.

Anyte 12: Geoghegan 10

The young dog was bitten by a viper hiding among the exposed roots of a bush.

Anyte 13: Geoghegan 11

The sound of the wings of a cricket or cicada used to wake the speaker in the morning. The "marauder" who killed the insect could be an animal or perhaps a child. The word for "claw" could also mean a human fingernail. Perhaps the child meant to catch it for a pet and killed it accidentally. Crickets were common pets (see 14).

Anyte 14: Geoghegan 20

A girl, Myro, weeps over the double grave of her pet cricket and cicada. The language here is purposely elevated. Insect epitaphs were very popular.

3–4. immovable Hades: The god of death is "hard to persuade" because he does not return what he has taken.

Anyte 15: Geoghegan 9

2. bloodied bay chest: The adjective can refer to the color ("bay") of the horse, its temperament ("bloody/warlike"), or bloodstains on its coat from itself or from men killed by its master, Damis.

4. ploughed soil: The soil is "difficult/troubled," which probably means soil that has been worked or ploughed; the battle took place in a ploughed field.

Anyte 16: Geoghegan 4

This epitaph for Captain Pheidias refers to the mourning of the young men who buried him and to the tombstone with this verse itself carved on it.

Anyte 17: Geoghegan 21

Anyte 18: Geoghegan 5
3. Philainis: Kleina's daughter, Philainis, died unmarried.
4. Acheron: Acheron is the river the dead cross to the underworld.

Anyte 19: Geoghegan 6
2. bridegrooms: The suitors of Antibia were all sure they would become her bridegroom.
3. wit: Antibia won high fame for her "wit" ("understanding" or "wisdom").

Anyte 20: Geoghegan 7
4. Thanatos: Death.

Anyte 21: Geoghegan 8
3. set a virgin: The mother of Thersis set a life-sized statue on her grave.
4. greeted: Thersis receives the statue and greetings at her grave instead of gifts and greetings at her wedding.

Anyte 22: EG 22

Although 22 and 23 are ascribed to Anyte, they are probably not by her.

This poem is about three young women who committed suicide rather than wait for murder or rape when the Gauls sacked their city.
2. lawless . . . godless: The Gauls rejected the laws of men and the gods.

Anyte 23: EG 23

Power only affects the living; once dead, the slave and the king are equals.
2. Darius: Probably Darius I, the king of Persia (521–486).

NOSSIS

Nossis, a Lokrian epigrammist, wrote in the early third century. Her poetry shows clear signs of Sappho's influence, although Nossis' love poems are lost. Her dialect is Doric with Sapphic Aeolicisms. Ten of Nossis' twelve epigrams speak from a female persona; in two poems she identifies herself as the speaker (1, 2). For an analysis of Nossis' use of Sappho as a poetic model, see Skinner (1989).

Epigrams 3–7 refer to dedications, 7–10 to portraits that may also be dedications. Nossis' epigrams were collected in the *Greek Anthology*.

Nossis 1: EG 1

1–2. That love is sweeter than honey may also refer to kinds of poetry. Skinner (1989) argues that "honey" song could refer to Pindaric praise-song, and "love" song to Sappho's poetry.

3–4. Aphrodite's kiss is both erotic and poetic: without her kiss of inspiration, one doesn't know what kind of roses her flowers are. Roses are a symbol both of the Muses' poetic gift and of Aphrodite's sexuality.

Nossis 2: EG 11

This epigram poses as a message from Nossis to Sappho's native city, Mitylene, addressed to anyone who may read the poem and pass the message on (Tarán, 146–49).

2. catch fire: The assumption is that the stranger goes to Mitylene to be inspired by Sappho's poetry, as Nossis clearly was.

Nossis 3: EG 2

Soldiers from Lokri dedicated to the gods shields captured from Bruttian men, from southwest Italy.

3–4. The shields are a personified testimony to the Lokrians' bravery: the shields praise the Lokrians and do not long for their former Bruttian owners.

Nossis 4: EG 3

The robe woven by Nossis and her mother Theuphilis was dedicated to Hera at her famous temple on the Lakinian promontory in southern Italy.

3. Kleocha's daughter Theuphilis: Greek women may have commonly used the female matronymic in addressing each other, rather than the formal delineation from the father; see Skinner (1987).

Nossis 5: EG 4

Polyarchis, a prostitute, was able to dedicate a statue of Aphrodite from her earnings.

Nossis 6: EG 5
4. Adonis: After Aphrodite's young lover, Adonis, was killed, she preserved his body with a nectar salve.

Nossis 7: EG 6

Nossis 8: EG 7
The portrait depicts Thaumareta so realistically that her own dog might mistake the picture for the person.

Nossis 9: EG 8
This portrait of Melinna has captured her essence.

Nossis 10: EG 9
3. wit: "Wisdom/understanding."

Nossis 11: EG 10
This is an epitaph to Rhinthon, who wrote thirty-eight burlesques of tragedy, including some of Euripides'.

Nossis 12: EG 12
There is some doubt that this is by Nossis. Artemis is the virgin huntress who helps women in childbirth.
1. Delos and Ortygia: Artemis was born on Ortygia and Apollo on Delos.
3. Inopos: She must wash off in the Delian stream after hunting, before helping Alketis deliver. Artemis here seems more an active midwife than a distant patron deity.

MOIRO

Moiro (Myro) lived in Byzantium in the third century. The first poem, in hexameters, and the two epigrams survive in quotations.

Moiro 1: Powell (p. 21)
Rhea hid her son Zeus on Krete to protect him from his father Kronos. Some doves and an eagle brought him ambrosia and nectar, the appropriate fare for an immortal baby. After Zeus had come to power by conquering his father, he honored the birds. The poem thus explains how the eagle came to be Zeus' immortal bird and how doves became the first sign of summer and winter. The

word for "doves" is the same as the word for the constellation Pleiades, whose rising and setting marks the change of seasons.

Moiro 2: Gow-Page 1

This epigram addresses a grape cluster that has been dedicated to Aphrodite.

2. Dionysos: The grapes are full of Dionysos' wine.

3–4. your mother: The cluster has been plucked from its mother grapevine to go to Aphrodite's temple.

Moiro 3: Gow-Page 2

1. As White (21–25) notes, all water and tree nymphs were considered daughters of Okeanos, the ocean that the Greeks pictured as a great river circling the earth.

2. depths: The nymphs wander the depths of the forest.

HEDYLA

Hedyla lived in Athens in the third century. This mythological poem in elegiac couplets refers to the unsuccessful wooing of Skylla by Glaukos (a merman). Skylla was a human woman whose rival in love turned her into a monster with six heads who preyed upon sailors. Hedyla's poem does not indicate Skylla's form. The poem survived as a quotation.

Hedyla 1: Supp. Hell. 456

1–3. Glaukos gives Skylla appropriate sea-gifts, shells and sea-bird chicks, but is "without hope" (literally, "distrustful") that the gifts will win her over—unless "distrustful" indicates that Skylla here is the monster, not the maiden.

4. Siren: Sirens are known for luring sailors to their death with their beautiful song, not for their compassion.

6. Aetna: Aetna (Etna) is a volcanic mountain in Sicily.

MELINNO

Melinno most likely lived in the first half of the second century. Her only surviving poem eulogizes the power of Rome. Each of the five Sapphic stanzas, in Doric dialect, ends with a complete stop, which lends a stiffness to the poem.

The goddess Roma is a deification of Rome and the Roman people in terms of a Hellenistic kingship. Many Greeks wrote poems about Roma, but few of the poems survive. For a thorough interpretation of the poem, see Bowra (1970, 199–212); for a study of the goddess Roma, see Mellor.

Melinno 1: Supp. Hell. 541

1–2. daughter of Ares: Roma and the Amazons are warlike daughters of Ares. Bowra suggests that Melinno is purposely describing Roma in terms of the Amazons. While *chryseomitra* ("gold-banded") usually means "with a golden headband," Bowra notes that with the Amazons it may refer to a "girdle/belt of gold," the symbol of their virgin power.

3–4. Olympos: Olympos is referred to as an unbreakable fortress of power and honor on earth. Roma lives on earth, not in the heavens.

5. Melinno emphasizes Rome's unique position of invulnerable strength by calling Roma an "eldest" goddess whose power was granted by Fate, and by repeating "you alone" in three of the five stanzas.

9–12. Roma yokes together earth and sea, "the cities of peoples," like a team of horses under her firm control. Hellenistic rulers demanded earth and water from conquered states as a sign of submission to their rule over land and sea.

13–16. While time changes everything else, Rome's power remains unchanging.

17–20. Rome produces warriors just as fertile earth produces crops.

Select Bibliography

Adkins, A. W. H. *Poetic Craft in the Early Greek Elegists*. Chicago: University of Chicago Press, 1985.

Allen, A., and J. Frel. "A Date for Corinna." *Classical Journal* 68 (1972): 26–30.

Ancher, G., B. Boyaval, and C. Meillier. "Etudes sur l'Egypte et le Soudan anciens." *Cahier de Recherches de l'Institut de Papyrologie et d'Egyptologie de Lille* 4 (1976): 255–360.

Arthur, M. B. "The Tortoise and the Mirror: Erinna *PSI* 1090." *Classical World* 74 (1980): 53–65.

Barnard, S. "Hellenistic Women Poets." *Classical Journal* 73 (1978): 204–13.

Barron, J. P. "Ibycus: To Polycrates." *Bulletin of the Institute of Classical Studies of the University of London* 16 (1969): 119–49.

Bowra, C. M. *Greek Lyric Poetry from Alcman to Simonides*. 2d ed. Oxford: Clarendon Press, 1961.

———. *On Greek Margins*. Oxford: Clarendon Press, 1970.

Bremer, J. M., A. M. van Erp Taalman Kip, and S. R. Slings. *Some Recently Found Greek Poems*. Leiden and New York: E. J. Brill, 1987.

Burnett, A. P. *Three Archaic Poets: Archilochus, Alcaeus, Sappho*. Cambridge, Mass.: Harvard University Press, 1983.

———. "Jocasta in the West: The Lille Stesichorus." *Classical Antiquity* 7 (1988): 107–54.

Calame, C. *Les choeurs de jeunes filles en grèce archaïque*. Vol. 2, *Alcman*. Rome: Edizioni dell'Ateneo & Bizzari, 1977.

———. *Alcman*. Rome: Edizioni dell'Ateneo & Bizzari, 1983.

Cambridge History of Classical Literature. Vol. 1, *Greek Literature*. Edited by P. E.

Easterling and B. M. W. Knox. Cambridge: Cambridge University Press, 1985.

Cameron, A., and A. Cameron. "Erinna's Distaff." *Classical Quarterly* n.s. 19 (1969): 285–88.

Campbell, D. A. *Greek Lyric Poetry: A Selection*. New York: St. Martin's Press, 1967.

———. *Greek Lyric*. Vol. 1, *Sappho, Alcaeus*. Cambridge, Mass.: Harvard University Press, 1982.

———. *The Golden Lyre: The Themes of the Greek Lyric Poets*. London: Duckworth, 1983.

Carson, A. *Eros the Bittersweet*. Princeton: Princeton University Press, 1986.

———. "Simonides Negative." *Arethusa* 21 (1988): 147–57.

Clayman, D. L. "The Meaning of Corinna's Ϝεροῖα." *Classical Quarterly* n.s. 28 (1978): 396–97.

Davison, J. A. *From Archilochus to Pindar*. New York: St. Martin's Press, 1968.

DeJean, Joan. *Fictions of Sappho, 1546–1937*. Chicago: University of Chicago Press, 1989.

Demand, N. *Thebes in the Fifth Century*. London and Boston: Routledge & Kegan Paul, 1982.

Dover, K. J. *Greek Homosexuality*. Cambridge, Mass.: Harvard University Press, 1978.

Dunkel, G. "Fighting Words: Alcman 'Partheneion' 63 μάχονται" *Indo-European Studies* 3 (1977): 249–72.

Easterling, P. E. "Alcman 58 and Simonides 37." *Proceedings of the Cambridge Philological Society* 200 (1974): 37–43.

Edmonds, J. M. *Lyra Graeca*. Vol. 1. Cambridge, Mass.: Harvard University Press, 1928.

Felson-Rubin, N. "Some Functions of the Enclosed Invective in Archilochus' Erotic Fragment." *Classical Journal* 74 (1978/79): 136–41.

Fränkel, H. *Early Greek Poetry and Philosophy*. Translated by M. Hadas and J. Willis. New York and London: Harcourt Brace Jovanovich, 1975.

Gentili, B. *Poetry and Its Public in Ancient Greece*. Baltimore and London: Johns Hopkins University Press, 1988.

Geoghegan, D. *Anyte: The Epigrams*. Rome: Edizioni dell'Ateneo & Bizzarri, 1979.

Gerber, D. E. *Euterpe*. Amsterdam: Hakkert, 1970.

———. "Studies in Greek Lyric Poetry: 1975–1985." Parts I, II. *Classical World* 81 (1987/88): 73–144, 417–79.

Giangrande, G. "An Epigram of Erinna." *Classical Review* n.s. 19 (1969): 1–3.

Gostoli, A. "Some Aspects of the Theban Myth in the Lille Stesichorus." *Greek, Roman, and Byzantine Studies* 19 (1978): 23–27.

Gow, A. S. F., and D. L. Page. *The Greek Anthology: Hellenistic Epigrams.* Vols. 1 and 2. Cambridge: Cambridge University Press, 1965.

Griffiths, A. "Alcman's Partheneion: The Morning After the Night Before." *Quaderni Urbinati di Cultura Classica* 14 (1972): 7–30.

Gutzwiller, K. J. *Studies in the Hellenistic Epyllion.* Germany: Verlag Anton Hain, 1981.

Hallett, J. P. "Sappho and Her Social Context: Sense and Sensuality." *Signs* 4 (1979): 447–64.

Haslam, M. "The Versification of the New Stesichorus (P. Lille 76abc)." *Greek, Roman, and Byzantine Studies* 19 (1978): 29–57.

Herington, J. *Poetry into Drama.* Berkeley and Los Angeles: University of California Press, 1985.

Irwin, E. *Colour Terms in Greek Poetry.* Toronto: Hakkert, 1974.

Johnson, W. R. *The Idea of Lyric.* Berkeley and Los Angeles: University of California Press, 1982.

Kirkwood, G. M. *Early Greek Monody.* Ithaca and London: Cornell University Press, 1974.

Lefkowitz, M. R. *The Lives of the Greek Poets.* Baltimore and London: Johns Hopkins University Press, 1981.

Lloyd-Jones, H., and P. Parsons. *Supplementum Hellenisticum.* Berlin: Walter de Gruyter, 1983.

Lobel, E. "2370. Corinna, Ϝεροίων ᾱ" *Oxyrhynchus Papyri*, vol. 23, 61–65. London: Egypt Exploration Society, 1956.

Lobel, E., and D. L. Page. *Poetarum Lesbiorum Fragmenta.* Oxford: Clarendon Press, 1955.

Marcovich, M. "Anacreon, 358 PMG." *American Journal of Philology* 104 (1983): 372–83.

Mellor, R. *Thea Rome: The Worship of the Goddess Roma in the Greek World.* Göttingen: Vandenhoeck & Ruprecht, 1975.

Miralles, C., and J. Portulas. *Archilochus and the Iambic Poetry.* Rome: Edizioni dell'Ateneo, 1983.

Most, G. W. "Greek Lyric Poets." In *Ancient Writers: Greece and Rome*, edited by T. J. Luce, vol. 1. New York: Scribner's Sons, 1982.

———. "Alcman's 'Cosmogonic' Fragment (Fr. 5 Page, 81 Calame)." *Classical Quarterly* 37 (1987): 1–19.

Nagy, G. *Comparative Studies in Greek and Indic Meter*. Cambridge, Mass.: Harvard University Press, 1974.

———. *The Best of the Achaeans*. Baltimore and London: Johns Hopkins University Press, 1979.

———. *Greek Mythology and Poetics*. Ithaca and London: Cornell University Press, 1990.

Page, D. L. *Alcman: The Partheneion*. New York: Arno Press, 1951.

———. *Corinna*. London: Society for the Promotion of Hellenic Studies, 1953.

———. *Sappho and Alcaeus*. Oxford: Clarendon Press, 1955.

———. *Poetae Melici Graeci*. Oxford: Clarendon Press, 1962.

———. "Stesichorus: The Geryoneïs." *Journal of Hellenic Studies* 93 (1973): 138–54.

———. *Supplementum Lyricis Graecis*. Oxford: Clarendon Press, 1974.

———. *Epigrammata Graeca*. Oxford: Clarendon Press, 1975.

Parsons, P. J. "The Lille 'Stesichorus'." *Zeitschrift für Papyrologie und Epigraphik* 26 (1977): 7–36.

———. "Recent Papyrus Finds: Greek Poetry." In *Actes du VIIᵉ Congrès de la Fédération Internationale des Associations d'Etudes Classiques*, edited by János Harmatta, vol. 2, 517–31. Budapest: Akadémiai Kiadó, 1984.

Podlecki, A. J. *The Early Greek Poets and Their Times*. Vancouver: University of British Columbia Press, 1984.

Pomeroy, S. B. "Supplementary Notes on Erinna." *Zeitschrift für Papyrologie und Epigraphik* 32 (1978): 17–28.

Powell, J. U. *Collectanea Alexandrina*. Oxford: Clarendon Press, 1925.

Rayor, D. J. "Translating Fragments." *Translation Review* 32–33 (1990): 15–18.

Renehan, R. "Anacreon Fragment 13 Page." *Classical Philology* 79 (1984): 28–32.

Segal, C. "Sirius and the Pleiades in Alcman's Louvre Partheneion." *Mnemosyne* 36 (1983): 260–75.

Skinner, M. B. "Briseis, The Trojan Women, and Erinna." *Classical World* 75 (1982): 265–69.

———. "Corinna of Tanagra and Her Audience." *Tulsa Studies in Women's Literature* 2 (1983): 9–20.

———. "Greek Women and the Metronymic: A Note on an Epigram by Nossis." *Ancient History Bulletin* 1 (1987): 39–42.

———. "Sapphic Nossis." *Arethusa* 22 (1989): 5–18.

Snodgrass, A. *Archaic Greece*. Berkeley and Los Angeles: University of California Press, 1980.

Snyder, J. M. "Korinna's 'Glorious Songs of Heroes'." *Eranos* 82 (1984): 125–34.

———. *The Woman and the Lyre*. Carbondale: Southern Illinois University Press, 1989.

Stigers, E. S. "Romantic Sensuality, Poetic Sense: A Response to Hallett on Sappho." *Signs* 4 (1979): 465–71.

———. "Sappho's Private World." In *Reflections of Women in Antiquity*, edited by H. P. Foley, 45–61. London and New York: Gordon and Breach Science Publishers, 1981.

Tarán, S. L. *The Art of Variation in the Hellenistic Epigram*. Leiden: E. J. Brill, 1979.

Van Sickle, J. "The New Archilochus Texts: Introduction." *Arethusa* 9 (1976): 133–47.

Voigt, E.-M. *Sappho et Alcaeus: Fragmenta*. Amsterdam: Athenaeum–Polak & Van Gennep, 1971.

West, M. L. "Alcmanica." *Classical Quarterly* 15 (1965): 188–202.

———. "Corinna." *Classical Quarterly* 20 (1970): 277–87.

———. "Stesichorus." *Classical Quarterly* 21 (1971): 302–14.

———. *Studies in Greek Elegy and Iambus*. New York: Walter de Gruyter, 1974.

———. "Erinna." *Zeitschrift für Papyrologie und Epigraphik* 25 (1977): 95–119.

———. "Stesichorus at Lille." *Zeitschrift für Papyrologie und Epigraphik* 29 (1978): 1–4.

———. *Delectus ex Iambis et Elegis Graecis*. Oxford: Clarendon Press, 1980.

White, H. *Essays in Hellenistic Poetry*. Amsterdam: J. C. Gieben, 1980.

Winkler, J. "Gardens of Nymphs: Public and Private in Sappho's Lyrics." In *Reflections of Women in Antiquity*, edited by H. P. Foley, 63–89. London and New York: Gordon and Breach Science Publishers, 1981.

———. *The Constraints of Desire*. New York and London: Routledge, 1990.

Numeration Table

ARCHILOCHOS

West	Rayor
1	1
5	3
13	6
19	10
30–31	15
105	8
114	2
115 Hipponax	9
118	18
122	7
128	4
130	5
174	11
176	12
177	13
191	17
193	16
196	19
201	14

SLG	
S 478	20

ALKMAN

PMG	Rayor
1	1
3	2
26	3
56	4
58	5
59	6
89	7

STESICHOROS

PMG	Rayor
187	1
192	3
209	4
223	2

SLG	
S 7–19	5

Bremer	
F	6

SAPPHO

Voigt	Rayor
1	1
2	2
5	44
15	38
16	4
17	3
22	9
23	10
27	53
30	61
31	8
33	11
34	7
37	40
39	6
41	13
42	30
44	51
44A (a–b)	50
47	19
48	24
49	35
50	41
51	65
52	21
54	22
55	33
56	12
57	34
58	29
63	26
71	37
81	5

Voight	Rayor
94	14
95	17
96	15
98 (a–b)	46
101 (a)	31
102	18
104 (a)	47
105 (a)	48
105 (b)	49
106	32
107	60
110	58
111	57
112	54
113	55
114	59
115	56
118	67
120	43
121	28
126	25
130 (a)	16
130 (b)	36
132	45
137	42
140	63
141	52
146	20
147	68
150	64
154	62
158	39
160	66
166	23
168 (b)	27

ALKAIOS

Voigt	Rayor
34	4
38 (a)	7
42	5
130 (b)	2
208	1
283	6
298	3
347	8

IBYKOS

PMG	Rayor
285	4
286	1
287	2
317 (a)	3

SLG	
S 151	5

ANAKREON

PMG	Rayor
346	11
348	2
356 (a–b)	1
357	3
358	4
360	5
376	6
395	10
398	7
413	8
417	9

SIMONIDES

PMG	Rayor
508	9
520	1
521	2
522	3
531	4
541	6
542	7
543	10
553	11
567	13
579	14
581	5
584	8
595	12

KORINNA

PMG	Rayor
654 col. i 12–34	2
654 col. iii 12–51	3
655	1
657	4
658	5
660	6
662	7
663	8
664 (a)	9
664 (b)	10
666	11
669	12
674	13
678	14
690	15

TELESILLA

PMG	Rayor
717	1

PRAXILLA

PMG	Rayor
747	1
748	2
749	3
750	4
754	5

ERINNA

Supp. Hell.	Rayor
401	1
402	2
404	3

Gow-Page	
1	4
3	6

Giangrande	
p. 1	5

ANYTE

Geoghegan	Rayor
1	1
2	2
3	3
4	16
5	18
6	19
7	20
8	21
9	15
10	12
11	13
12	11
13	9
14	10
15	5
16	7
17	6
18	8
19	4
20	14
21	17

EG	
22	22
23	23

NOSSIS

EG	Rayor
1	1
2	3
3	4
4	5
5	6
6	7
7	8
8	9
9	10
10	11
11	2
12	12

MOIRO

Powell	Rayor
p. 21	1

Gow-Page	
1	2
2	3

HEDYLA

Supp. Hell.	Rayor
456	1

MELINNO

Supp. Hell.	Rayor
541	1

Designer:	Barbara Jellow
Compositor:	Wilsted & Taylor
Text:	11/14 Galliard
Display:	Galliard
Printer:	Maple-Vail Book Manufacturing Group
Binder:	Maple-Vail Book Manufacturing Group